INDIA IN THE BALANCE

INDIA IN THE BALANCE

BRITISH RULE AND THE CALIPHATE

KHWAJA KAMAL-UD-DIN, B. A., LL.B

Published by

Gyan Publishing House
5, Ansari Road
Daryaganj, New Delhi-110002
Phone: 011-47034999, 9811692060
E-mail: books@gyanbooks.com

Distribution Network
gyanbooks.com
India, USA, Canada, UK, Australia, France

ISBN: 978-81-212-8812-5 (PB)
First Published, 1922

2nd Impression 2023

Printed at: Gyan Press, Delhi.

INDIA IN THE BALANCE
Author: Khwaja Kamal-Ud-Din

INDIA IN THE BALANCE

INDIA IN THE BALANCE

BRITISH RULE AND THE CALIPHATE

BY

KHWAJA KAMAL-UD-DIN, B.A., LL.B.

IMAM OF THE MOSQUE, WOKING

AUTHOR OF "THE SECRET OF EXISTENCE," "THE IDEAL PROPHET," "REVELATION A NECESSITY," ETC., ETC.

"THE ISLAMIC REVIEW"

THE MOSQUE, WOKING

FOREWORD

In all the course of my public career I have never, till now, touched politics. Rather have I purposely avoided them as forming a topic apart, with a tendency to create false perspectives when applied to matters outside its own particular, and somewhat narrow, sphere. For the last ten years, since relinquishing my practice at the Bar, I have devoted my whole time to religion, which, of all subjects, has been generally considered that most distinctly set apart from politics. Yet the war, in its course of destruction, has not spared even this intangible barrier, and to-day the line of demarcation between religion and politics is lost.

To many in East and West alike, but especially in the East, religion is still a very real and living thing; and when we find religion openly used as something more than a pawn in the dubious game of politics, we must needs find also—be we of Europe or Asia—food for disquieting thought.

The eyes of India to-day are watching the

first-fruits of this new departure, as revealed in the problem of the Caliphate and the integrity of the Turkish Empire; for the handier solution of which the principles of the Faith of Islam are being called in question, and Muslim doctrines deliberately misrepresented by pro-Greek propaganda for a political purpose—professing to show that it is impossible for a Christian race to live unmolested under Muslim rule. Unfortunately, grave misconceptions as to the Faith of Islam and what it stands for, are still widely prevalent in England. Recent developments in the Near East and elsewhere have, it is true, induced the British Government to lend a belated ear to Muslim claims; but the root of the trouble must be sought in the indifference of the British people to Muslim susceptibilities, which indifference is largely due to inaccurate and meagre information.

Nor is such an attitude difficult to understand, when the alleged experts and self-constituted authorities on Eastern affairs, who write *ex cathedra* in the leading journals, and upon whom devolves the task of making and moulding public opinion, are themselves ignorant of the true significance of the phenomena of which they write.

My sole object in this little book is to put fairly and squarely before the people of Great

Britain the actual position to-day of the people of India.

I shall endeavour to state, dispassionately and without bias, the condition of Muslim feeling in India as it is, and its possible bearings on the future; and, having stated the case as it is, neither justifying nor condemning, and explained the why and the wherefore, I shall ask the people of Great Britain to judge and, having judged, to see to it that their judgment is translated into action.

During the ten years in which I have been in direct touch with English people in England, my impression of the English has changed greatly. It is now, I had almost said, fundamentally different from what it used to be—and what it is still apt to be, I am afraid, when I am in India; and it is to that innate English sense of justice, honesty and fair play, which I find everywhere in this country, that I confidently appeal.

And here I may remark that the ideal of a united India, about which we have been reading so much of late, is not without practical difficulties for Indians, be they Muslim or Hindu.

The vast populations involved—aggregating some seventy millions of the one and two hundred and thirty millions of the other—

render the process of welding them into any sort of genuine corporate union, one that involves time, together with infinite patience and mutual understanding before all things. And, further, there is the danger, equally present and equally repugnant to both, that in such fusion—as in a melting-pot—distinctions of race and tradition and custom, and, indeed, everything that makes for national individuality, equally precious to both—may become lost.

Such an ideal of ultimate union is cherished as an ideal, by educated Indians, Muslim and Hindu alike; but the "melting-pot" looms ahead, and it is the fear of the "melting-pot" which has hitherto kept the two races apart. I say "hitherto," for circumstances are like to prove too strong for the millions who have hesitated, and are still hesitating, reluctant to take the first decisive step on a perilous path that leads they know not whither, but impelled thereto more and more by mysterious forces from the West.

For this is a mystery—to me, at least.

At the present time every English official entrusted with the task of Indian government in India, from the Viceroy and the Governors of Presidencies and Provinces downwards, through every branch of the administration, is convinced that the trouble is due, as regards

Muslims at least, to a feeling of real and desperate anxiety arising from the provisions of the Treaty of Sèvres as affecting the Caliphate and the integrity of Turkey, and that such anxiety is justified and should be removed.

The Home Government, too, on the occasion of the publication of the Viceroy's now famous message and Mr. Montagu's consequent resignation, stated expressly that that resignation was necessitated by the unauthorized action of the late Secretary of State, and was not to be construed as indicating the Government's want of sympathy in any way with the purport of the message.

All parties would seem to be agreed—yet nothing is done.

It would be palpably a foolish thing to suggest any doubt whatsoever as to the *bona fides* either of the Indian Administration, or of the Government at home.

What, then, is the reason? There can be, as I believe, but one; and that one, that even now the Home Government, at least, is not fully alive to the real urgency of things in India; and it is in this belief, and in the earnest hope that a full and accurate knowledge of the actual position will, even at the eleventh hour, convince the British people and the British Government of the ever-gathering peril of delay, that I have written this book. Now is the time to act. The thing has not yet gone too far, but if action be over-long delayed, an inevitable step will have been taken which, whatever may be its immediate and ultimate effects on Hindu and Muslim destinies, can scarcely fail to result in an outlook new and sinister for British rule in India.

CONTENTS

CHAPTER		PAGE
	FOREWORD	5
I.	THE MUSLIM CONCEPTION OF GOVERNMENT	13
II.	THE CHANGE AND ITS CAUSES IN GENERAL	25
III.	THE PAST AND PRESENT ATTITUDE OF THE MUSLIM IN INDIA	32
IV.	THE CHANGE IN THE MUSLIMS	39
V.	AFTER THE TREATY OF SÈVRES	46
VI.	INCENDIARISM AND THE GOVERNMENT'S DRASTIC MEASURES	56
VII.	THE CALIPHATE	73
VIII.	THE CALIPHATE AND THE LAND OF PILGRIMAGE	86
IX.	MUSLIM INTERESTS IN PALESTINE	105
X.	THE CALIPHATE AND ITS CLAIMANTS	114
XI.	NON-MUSLIMS UNDER MUSLIM RULE	131
XII.	CONCLUSION	151

PAGE

APPENDIX I. THE PENALTY FOR APOSTASY IN ISLAM 164

" II. THE ANATOLIAN VILLAGES BURNT BY THE HELLENIC ARMY . 169

" III. THE MINORITIES . . . 170

" IV. WRITTEN STATEMENT OF MAHATMA GANDHI . . . 171

" V. CHRISTIAN OFFICIALS IN THE TURKISH ADMINISTRATION . 176

INDIA IN THE BALANCE

CHAPTER I

THE MUSLIM CONCEPTION OF GOVERNMENT

THE ignorance that exists in England concerning Islam may be of the kind that arises rather from lack of opportunity than of desire to learn, but its extent is amazing; more especially when it is remembered that the Muslim subjects of His Majesty outnumber the Christian. Hence, the strangest allegations and the most grotesque of fairy tales—appalling and diverting by turns—are received without suspicion, and pass lightly into alleged fact, which is, of course, ample ground for any charge or theory, however extraordinary.

There is, for example, a widely entertained idea—almost subconscious at times—that this Muslim civilization, if such it can be called, is at best a wild and exotic thing. Mahdis and Mad Mullahs, dervish hordes and marauding Bedouin, and the moving incidents of their exploits, wherein savage scenery and unaccustomed garb serve to enhance the inevitable horrors of even border warfare, have doubtless had their effect on the man in the street—filling the stage of his mind when the Eastern curtain rings up, to the exclusion of the millions of Muslims, every whit as peaceable as himself, who, with him, constitute the audience.

It is easy to visualize a sufficiently vivid and convincing whole from an insignificant part, if that part be dramatic, not to say picturesque; but it is not fair, neither is it particularly wise.

Before we judge a cause or a system—be it a civilization or some lesser thing—it is surely as well to know what it is; and before we make up our minds to the fact that the Muslim is, as such, a turbulent and irresponsible creature with an embarrassing turn for blood—the Ishmael of world-politics, with his hand against every man and, by reason of the nature of such civilization as is his, constitutionally impatient of control—it would be only fair to inquire as to this same civilization, and find out for ourselves what actually is the Muslim conception of government.

There is an anecdote (historical) of the great Omar, the second of the Caliphs, which seems to me to the point.

One Jabala, king of the Ghassanides, a recent convert to Islam, whilst performing the *tawaf*, or circumambulation of the Kaaba, became annoyed with a humble pilgrim engaged in the same pious duty, because the latter had inadvertently permitted a portion of his pilgrim's dress to come in contact with the royal person. Jabala struck the man, knocking out his teeth, and the victim came to the great Caliph for redress. "I sent for Jabala," wrote the Caliph to one of his generals, "and asked him why he had so ill-treated a brother Muslim. He answered that the man had insulted him, and that were it not for the sanctity of the place he would have killed him on the spot. I replied that his words added to the gravity of the offence, and that unless he obtained the pardon of the injured man he would have to submit to the usual penalty of the law. Jabala replied, 'I am a king, and the other is only a common man.'" To which Omar made answer, "King or no king, both of you are Mussulmans, and *both of you are equal in the eyes of the law.*" Jabala duly fled to escape the degradation of the penalty; but the words of Omar remain the ultimate summing up of the Muslim ideal of government—which is to say, democracy in its most human form.

Such was, and is, the law's regard for the individual, and that of the individual for the law is like unto it. Remember that we are judging Muslim law as we should British—by its principles, and not by breaches of those principles.

Muslim reverence for authority is instilled from earliest childhood. "And your Lord has commanded," says the Qur-án, "that you shall not serve others than Him, and that to your parents you shall do good; if either or both of them reach old age with you . . . do not grumble at them, but speak to them respectfully. And lower to them the wing of humility out of compassion and say, 'O Lord, have compassion on them, even as they brought me up when I was little'" (xvii. 23, 24). So also the rule of conduct for those of riper years is explicit enough: "Obey God and the Apostle and those who re in authority among you."

Authority is to be obeyed, and the person as representing authority. Such a person may be of any religion, but as parents are to be obeyed so must he be obeyed, and that he profess, or not, the Muslim faith is neither here nor there. There is a tradition that the Prophet ordained that this duty of obedience must not be withheld even from a negro slave; and though, in these latter days, such ordinances may be considered to err on the side of too great strictness, yet it will scarcely be denied that they do indicate a species of civilization peculiarly amenable to just and ordered government.

Such, then, is the attitude of the Muslim—the Indian Muslim as well as his brethren of the Faith—towards government by his own people; and if it be asked how this differs from his attitude towards British government, the answer will be—not at all.

The principle involved in the words of Omar is still uppermost in the mind of every thinking Muslim, for democracy—practicable and practical—is no new idea with us, as it is with you in the West. Democracy in its present form had its birth and home in Islam. This may appear a strong claim, but the seven principles promulgated by the Qur-án and the Prophet to constitute a democratic rule, which I give below, will substantiate my assertion, and those who, actuated by Turcophobia, say that the Turkish rule, based on the Qur-ánic lines, cannot suit the present progressive communities, should think twice before they make such absurd remarks. It only shows their ignorance. I challenge them to show us better basic principles of rule than those laid down by Islam.

Muslims possess their own jurisprudence, the best basic principles of law of which a civilization can boast. The source of this law is the Qur-án—a book from God, and not a product of the human brain which is incapable of keeping pace with the needs of humanity from age to age. Now, I give these principles.

Firstly, sovereign political authority, for which the word Khilafat (Caliphate) stands in the Qur-án, and in the traditions of the Prophet. The word no doubt includes religious authority also, but this religious aspect I shall deal with fully in a subsequent chapter.

Secondly, the person representing sovereign political authority, or Caliphate. There are several ways in which a person may become Caliph; but the most commendable one is *election*.

Thirdly, the Caliph cannot rule without consulting the ruled. The famous dictum of the Caliph Omar sums up this principle clearly enough. "There can be no Khilafat," he says, "unless the voice of the ruled is respected." The Qur-án also enjoins upon the king that he is to take counsel in state affairs: "And take counsel with them in the affairs" (iii. 158).

Fourthly, the king should rule for the benefit of the ruled, and not for his personal aggrandizement. "Blessed is He," the Qur-án says, "in whose hand is the kingdom, and He has power over all things. . . . He may try you—which of you *is best in deeds*" (lxvii. 1, 2). "It may be that your Lord will destroy your enemy, and make you ruler in the land, then He will see *how you act*" (vii. 129). "Then He made you successors (kings) in the land after them, so that We may see *how you act.*" "How you act" is the Divine test which must be satisfied before a nation is allowed by the Lord to continue to rule. Nations that do evil are swept away, and others are raised in their place, that they may do good. They live only so long as they do more good than harm to humanity, be they Muslims or non-Muslims; but when they begin to devote their lives to luxury and to indulge in evil, decay overtakes them. Thus the ruler has to rule for the benefit of the ruled, and not for his own benefit, or the benefit of his own nation, if he chance to have other races under him. The policy of weakening subject races by division and thereby strengthening his own nation is a most undesirable policy for a ruler, according to the teachings of the Qur-án.

Speaking of Pharaoh, the Qur-án says:

> Surely Pharaoh exalted himself in the land and made its people into parties, and weakening one party from among them . . . surely he was one of the mischief-makers (xxviii. 4).

Even in the tradition of the Prophet, speaking of the Quraishite Caliphate, to which prominence has of late been given by certain writers in the daily Press, the words of the Hadis very clearly lay down that the Caliphate in the Quraishite will continue only so long as they shall rule for the benefit of the ruled.

Fifthly, the Qur-án inspires a strong sense of submission to authority, and speaks of sedition as a wicked thing. The verse speaking against sedition is as follows: "God forbids indecency, and evil, and rebellion" (xvi. 90).

Sixthly, the governed must point out to the ruler, though with all respect, the defects and injustices in his government. The first sermon the Caliph Abu Bakr gave on the very first day of his power speaks of this right of the subject to criticize the ruler. "Put me in the right," the noble Caliph says, "if you find me in error." We have heard here a good deal of late of the Muslim Holy War, or *Jehad*, and it would seem to be regarded variously as one of the irresponsible ebullitions characteristic of a civilization in the nursery stage, or as a devastating eruption of fanatical ignorance; but the Prophet Muhammad himself said that the best form of *Jehad* is to approach the king, with the respect due to his kingship, and boldly tell him when he has committed a wrong.

Just as in British law, the appeal unto Cæsar —broadened from its Roman basis—has ever been the right, in principle, even of the humblest citizen, so access to authority, for the purpose of making known an injustice or obtaining redress for a grievance, is part and parcel of the law of Islam.

Seventhly, justice and equity, recognizing no distinction of descent or race, should characterize the rule. I have cited the case of King Jabala in this connection.

Those progressive nations who think that the Turkish rule, with the Qur-án as the basis of its legislation, is unfit to govern, will do well to ponder on the principles I have enumerated, which are the foundation of that rule. Can they conceive of better jurisprudence; or can they doubt but that, if these seven principles were consistently practised by ruling nations towards subject races, all the unrest which is at the present time manifesting itself in subject races everywhere would, as if by magic, disappear?

To emphasize the principle of submission to authority, sedition against the rule has not only been strongly prohibited, but it has also been hinted that if the governed found the rule too hard for him to submit to it, he would do better to leave the place under the said rule, rather than plot rebellion against it.

Herein, I think, is illustrated one striking and peculiar experience or privilege, call it what you will, which Islam alone has possessed of all world-faiths that have sprung from humble beginnings; to wit, that it has fallen to the lot of Islam to attain to temporal power so rapidly that its first Caliphs, within less than a generation of the Prophet's death —with the light of the spiritual dawn still upon them—were able to put their newly revealed principles of conduct to the proof in the greater matters of the world as well as in the less, thus demonstrating to all mankind their practical application, nationally as well as individually. Omar's words promptly involved him in war with the aggrieved monarch, but they proved that his faith was not an empty thing, nor one of implied limitations.

Foreign rule is not, of itself, obnoxious to the Muslim, and British rule in India during the last two centuries has been in no way discordant with Muslim ideas or with the Muslim faith.

The king, in whose person is symbolized authority, must, as king, have one religion only, and that justice—a conception closely analogous to the English maxim, "The king can do no wrong." British dominion being taken as a just dominion and one based on democracy found favour with Indian Muslims—*a fortiori* the fact that it is also, nominally at least, a Christian dominion, tended, if anything, to enhance that feeling. Here the man in the street may open his eyes, but it is true none the less, and for a very obvious and good reason.

Both the Christian faith and that of the Jews are regarded by the Qur-án as equally near akin to Islam. All three have the same Semitic origin, all three possess in common certain basic principles, and, while the prophets of Israel have their place in the Islamic hierarchy (if such a term be permissible), the Founder of Christianity is given the same reverence by Muslims as the Prophet himself.

But the consideration which outweighed all others with Muslim India lies in the fact that British government, though it be a government by a Christian power, was not a Christian government in the sense in which the rule of subject races by the Romans constituted

Roman government. That is to say, British rule had not sought in any way to force itself on the religion or the customs of the governed.

Events of the last twenty years in the Near East—and elsewhere—have, however, caused acute disappointment and a certain foreboding.

Up to that time Muslim India was content—having no apprehensions for the morrow.

Now, it is wondering.

CHAPTER II

THE CHANGE AND ITS CAUSES IN GENERAL

THE spirit of India is changed. The "pathetic content" deplored by Mr. Montagu has gone, and the wonder to which it has given place is ever growing. One factor in the situation —of some significance—must not be lost sight of. India, more especially during the last half-century, has visited England and has learnt to understand.

England for the last two centuries has been in India and has not learnt to understand.

The Anglo-Indian population—narrow, "exclusive," caste-ridden to an extent at which a Brahmin might blush—jogs complacently along, in the rut of what it conceives to be old tradition, forgetting—or not perceiving—that the rut has widened to a well-trodden highway, and oblivious of the fact that its own personnel is different from that of the builders of British India and their fellows, in just the same degree that competitive-examination efficiency differs from statecraft or mere brains from breeding.

To jog along on a broad highway, in the belief that it is a rut, may well excite the mirth of those that pass by; but when the joggers-on are persons in authority (however brief), who cannot see the joke or even admit that there is one, the mirth is apt to be tempered by inconvenience, not to say annoyance, and the mixture is not good.

But India has been to England too, and has learnt in English school and English university those old traditions that survive there yet. India has gone thence into the European world and seen for itself the manner in which those traditions are respected and upheld. India has been treated hospitably, with friendship and cordiality, as an honoured equal, and has returned, puzzled enough at all she has learnt, and particularly puzzled to find herself reduced, on a sudden, to a plane of racial inferiority.

And what has been the result of India's visit to England?

She has seen a country wherein all men are educated—where political power is for every class of the community, and, in theory, the knowledge how to use it. She has seen a nation more deeply stirred by the result of a race, a football match, or a boxing competition, than by an event of international import—concentrating its mental acumen on the prospects of the coming cricket season, rather than on the outcome of the crisis to which their Empire is drifting daily.

The Indian is puzzled thereby, not as yet realizing perhaps the extent to which familiarity may breed contempt, nor reflecting, as yet, that it is this kind of familiarity, the familiarity with the things that matter, that constitutes democracy's most real danger. Instead, he sees these to him priceless privileges of responsibility and citizenship held as of less than no account, and is frankly envious, and, it may be, a little uncomplimentary in thought towards these people that know not what they do.

I am not defending this attitude ; I merely suggest that it is an intelligible one.

Still more is the Indian at a loss when, after receiving with admiration and reverence the British gospel of equality for all, regardless of race, colour or religion, and observing it in actual operation, he returns to his native land to find between himself and his English fellow-citizens a great gulf fixed.

A cynic once observed that when a mixed boatload of English and Indians leaves Tilbury for Bombay there is, at the start, nothing to distinguish it from any other harmonious assemblage of equally civilized persons. Opinions differ as to the precise period of the voyage when the first signs of a cleavage begin to be perceptible, but all authorities are agreed that when Aden is left behind the thing is evident, and what was one community has become two.

Again, I do not contend that this should not be so. All may still be for the best in the best of all possible worlds, but to the Indian it is a little difficult to reconcile with theory on any grounds other than humiliating. He realizes—or thinks he realizes—and through him, in time, the India with which he comes in contact begins to realize, that the principles of English democracy may be, and very possibly are, excellent in themselves, and well suited to English people, but that they are not thought to be so suited to Indians.

That is the situation—to date.

There is no party in India that is really anxious to see the end of British rule. The resentment, if such it can be called, is not against the British Raj, but simply against present methods of administration. The turmoil and unrest which are, unhappily, everywhere in evidence are not the outcome of sedition, privy conspiracy, and rebellion; they are simply the admittedly imperfect methods of an inarticulate people to draw attention to an urgent need.

India feels that, in England, she is not understood.

Knowing that little may be hoped for from the Anglo-Indian element, she has pinned her faith to the English. She has appealed to England—and England is indifferent, or, at least, does not seem to care.

One example will suffice—a trivial episode in English estimation, but one of vast significance to India. Thirty years ago a newspaper was established for the purpose, if possible, of enlightening English opinion on the subject of Indian "aspirations" (I must apologize for using ex-President Wilson's foolish and rather mischievous phrase, but it serves to indicate my meaning). It was founded by the late Sir Henry Cotton and continued by his son: it was called *The Indian National Congress*, was published, throughout, in England, and, after thirty years' struggle, has just died of inanition. Nobody read it. Nobody cared.

India at last realizes the hopelessness of English propaganda—that it is in truth to fight "as one that beateth the air," and has determined at last, being compelled thereto, to work out her own salvation at home, as best she may.

If one fourth part of the rights and responsibilities that have been so freely lavished on England's illiterate, who have scarcely a "thank you" to spare for them, had been bestowed upon Indians in India, that fourth part would have made all the difference. India is lacking neither in education nor in what is called culture; nor yet in the finer perception that makes culture a valuable thing. Indian judges have proved not unworthy of the highest traditions of the English Courts, and, logically, there is no position, from Viceroy downwards, which an Indian is not adequately qualified to fill.

I have pointed out that one of the strongest factors in the stability of British government in India hitherto has been that it is government by Christians, rather than a Christian government. But now an idea is abroad that this government by Christians is ruling as a Christian government, and not as an impartial administration—favouring Christians, Christian interests and enterprises, to the prejudice of the religions of the country.

It is possible to make allowance for concessions to missionaries—the building of churches and religious institutions, and similar forms of activity, not unreasonable in themselves, but the war would seem to have shown—if we are to trust the published and acknowledged utterances of certain statesmen—that the ideal for which the Allies have fought—in the East, at any rate—is Christianity against all other creeds. When one eminent speaker referred to Salonika as the portal of Christendom, and another compared the British occupation of Jerusalem to the Crusades, India became on the instant suspicious and alert.

A thoughtless word, dropped in the fervour of political eloquence, may, at the worst, sow the seed of an embarrassing harvest; at the least it may convey a wrong impression, capable of being removed.

Is this impression a wrong one? If so, let something be done to show it; if, on the other hand, it is right—then the future is dark indeed.

CHAPTER III

THE PAST AND PRESENT ATTITUDE OF THE MUSLIMS IN INDIA

EVEN so late as 1912, the Muslims in India did not swerve an inch from their support of the government. The clear teaching of the Qur-án and the precepts of the Holy Prophet had engendered in them the spirit of true loyalty to the British rule. With the partition of Bengal, under Lord Curzon, serious unrest was created in that province, the whole of which was seething with anarchy—to such an extent, indeed, that the seat of government had to be changed from Calcutta to Delhi in consequence. Even then, support to the Government measure was still forthcoming from the Muslims. In fact, the whole of Bengal was split into two camps, Bengalees on the one side and the Government and the Muslims on the other. The outlook for the general well-being of the country was not a bright one. Amity between Hindu and Muslim, on certain lines, is essential for the welfare of India—a fact which was insisted upon by no less a person than the King himself at the Delhi Durbar in January 1912. The relations between the two races had become strained almost to breaking-point. It was clear that the state of things thus created could not go further. It began to affect the administration as well. The partition of the province was then annulled, and a homily of peace and unity preached at the Delhi Durbar. This was well enough, but the effect on the two communities was most deplorable, and promised to be lasting. The Hindus felt themselves in the position of the victors, and the Muslims of the vanquished. Then it dawned upon the former that something more than political agitation was necessary to secure the desired end; while the Muslims began to realize that to side with the government against their own countrymen could only bring shame and disgrace. Even in the very days of the Durbar the crestfallen Muslim leaders began to ask themselves what they should do now. The dissatisfaction was not confined to Bengal, but made itself felt in every corner of India, especially in the Punjab, where unrest among the Hindus had already begun to show itself in 1905, and had become acute in 1907. The leaders of the Muslim community in Lahore, the seat of the Punjab Government, thought it necessary to do something to keep their fellow-Muslims within proper limits. I was asked to deliver a series of lectures on the very subject which was agitating the leaders of Islam at the time of the Durbar. What should the Muslims do now?

In each lecture I dwelt upon a particular phase of the subject. The theme of the last lecture, which was listened to with rapt attention by an assembly of about five thousand persons, was "The Attitude of Muslims towards the British Government and other Muslim and non-Muslim Powers." The lecture appeared in one of the Indian journals, and I make the following few extracts from it simply to show how strong was the sense of submission to rule held by the Muslims in those days.

> The Maulawis (Muslim priests) have not forgotten the verse which the Holy Prophet made a point of reciting every Friday in his sermon from the pulpit, and which is consequently recited this day. The verse runs thus: "Verily God enjoineth justice, the doing of good and the giving unto kindred; and He forbiddeth immorality, wrong and revolt." . . . You will find by reference to the second part of the above verse that it deals with the very three matters to which the aforesaid laws refer . . . The first thing forbidden in the verse is *Fahsha*, which signifies such evil deeds as pertain to the personal morals of men. The next thing forbidden is *Munker*, i.e. such acts as involve a wrong to our fellow-creatures. Lastly, we are commanded not to resist the laws of the government, which have been framed to protect the rights

of the subjects. The word *Baghy* (revolt) is a comprehensive term which not only includes the sense of the word "sedition," but also applies to all those acts which are calculated to threaten the stability of a government established by law in a country.

Dealing with the first part of the verse, which enjoins the observance of three moral laws, I made the following remarks to show their application as regards the government:

If we respect the laws of the government and pay the legal taxes, we are not laying the government under any obligation. The government made laws for us and protected our lives, property and honour. . . . The Holy Qur-án requires us not to stop here, but to do more than this. But we should also practise beneficence in our relation with the government. . . . We should share the burden of our government, fly to its assistance when it is confronted with difficulties, create facilities for it, chastise its enemies and volunteer our services when it has to undertake great expeditions. . . . But the Holy Qur-án requires us to rise higher than this . . . showing that pure form of kindness which one shows to one's kinsmen (the last moral which the verse speaks of). . . . When a mother, for instance, lavishes her care on her child, she does not do so out of any desire for regard or recognition. We shall be practising this highest virtue in relation to the government if we render it services even without its knowledge and without looking for any reward from it. . . .

Referring to the unrest of 1907 in the Punjab, I said the following:

Ye thousands of men, that are now assembled in this meeting, and that are the residents of this great city, I ask you whether any seditious spirit was to be found in you in 1907, and whether you were so disloyal as to plot against authorities? Had you forgotten the teachings of the Qur-án with regard to obedience and loyalty? Had the verse recited to you from the pulpit every Friday faded from your memory? . . . You are Muslims, and no Muslim can be guilty of treachery; you are a believer, and no believer can wish evil to his rulers. You are the followers of the Holy Qur-án, and the Holy Qur-án enjoins obedience to authority on its followers. . . .

Referring to the conduct of the Muslims in those days, I said:

There is hardly any part of India which has been free from political agitation and intrigue during the past few years. Anarchism had appeared in various forms, and in every district affected was a large number of Muhammadans. East Bengal, some parts of which had been the centres of political agitation, has more Muhammadans than Hindus. . . . Why is it, then, that never a Muslim was involved in any of the intrigues, riots, dacoity, thefts and outrages that had been the order of the day during the past few years in every part of India? . . . It is to Islam and its Holy Founder . . . that the credit is really due for the admirable attitude of the Muslims towards their foreign ruler. . . .

Speaking about Pan-Islamism, I said:

The German and the Italian clergy are attempting the wholesale destruction of Islam by spreading the supposed terror under the name of Pan-Islamism. If by Pan-Islamism I am to understand that all Muslims living in the different parts of the earth are planning to overthrow the Christian empires, and thus to renew afresh the glory of Islam, it is a falsehood which has been made by mischiefmongers. . . . Religion is nothing but obedience to certain commandments . . . among other things, the order relating to submission to the government. It is an odd inconsistency that in endeavouring to live in the service of my religion I should wantonly allow myself to go against the express commandments of it. . . . But if Pan-Islamism means that the Muslim should wish that all the human souls living on earth may become Muslims and accept the truth of the Arabian Prophet, then I shall be the first to be proud of my love for Pan-Islamism !

The lecture was a very long one: it took me three hours to deliver it. It was heard with rapt attention, without exciting any question or arousing any opposition. That it went to the heart of the audience and mirrored their feeling can easily be ascertained from the fact that very full reports appeared in many vernacular papers, including the *Zamindar* of Lahore, the editor of which has now been considered as an arch-seditionist and is in jail. Only ten years have passed since then, and what a world of change is to-day in the Muslim attitude towards the British government. Suffice it to say that an utterance such as this of mine that I have quoted will not only barely secure the one-hundredth part of the audience in these days, but that if anyone went to the platform with such a lecture he would be hooted down. Who can wonder? How this change of feeling occurred is not a secret to the official class, or to the Government here; but to the millions of my fellow-subjects in this country it is still a mystery, and in the coming chapter I shall try to explain it briefly.

CHAPTER IV

THE CHANGE IN THE MUSLIMS

WITH the outbreak of war in 1914 the gathering murmurs of unrest were lost, for the time, in the din of a world-conflict, upon the upshot of which depended the future of every part of the British Empire, India included; and it was not until the entry of Turkey into the struggle that any cloud of difficulty began to hover in the horizon of Indian affairs.

Even then, by prompt and diplomatic handling, those on the spot who had some knowledge of Muslim feeling, and, in consequence, some glimmerings of the complications rendered possible by Turkey's action, succeeded in reconciling the duty required of Muslims, as subjects of the King-Emperor, with the allegiance due to the Sultan as Caliph, Guardian of the Holy Places and temporal representative of the spiritual entity called Islam. Turkey, they said with perfect truth, had deliberately elected to throw in her lot with the enemies of the British Government. It was not deemed necessary to go into the reasons which had moved Turkey to take such a step, repugnant as it was to the tradition of a hundred years and more; but, the step being taken, Turkey must be fought, brought to see the error of her ways, and received back eventually into the fold, chastened and penitent. Indian Muslims need entertain no qualms about waging war, ostensibly, with the temporal Head of their religion—for the whole dispute was of a purely political nature, without religious or spiritual significance of any kind.

Muslim India took them at their word. Blood and treasure flowed freely for Great Britain against the Turk. Such was the still surviving confidence in British good faith, which could induce a nation of Muslims to take arms against the temporal Head of their religion.

It was, none the less, a situation without precedent, involving points of unusual delicacy.

That it should have been capable of successful adjustment at all, and that with a minimum of friction and misunderstanding, was, indeed, in view of the highly controversial nature of the business, matter for congratulation for the adjusters, but could not warrant their losing sight for an instant of its essential peculiarities, which were, of course, still in being.

As with every compromise, there was an implied bargain. How far, with the best of good will, this was ever really capable of fulfilment on the British side is another question. So long, however, as that good will was present, and beyond suspicion, one might hope for the best.

The Indian had, in effect, to double the parts of enmity and amity—to fight for his country and maintain at the same time a sentiment of undiminished fraternity for the foe against whom he fought—to harmonize as best he could the sacred feeling of brotherhood with the clash of steel and the roar of the guns; for it must be remembered that the defeat of Turkey, to whatever extent justifiable, was bound to be felt in India. So the Indian troops fought gallantly, as all the world knows, and loyally kept their part of the bargain.

Then gradually, almost imperceptibly, something began to leak out—such is the mystical power of rumour in India—was all over that country before a hint of the truth had so much as suggested itself to that vast unofficial part of Great Britain, which still regards questions of public obligation and private honour as, in principle at least, analogous.

The rumour, which purported to give for the first time the real reason which forced Turkey to ally herself with the Central Powers, seemed on its merits outrageous enough, but doubly so when viewed in the light of that understanding to which I have just alluded.

The promise of Constantinople as a sop to Russia, for the purpose of dissuading that never too reliable ally from the project of a separate peace, might conceivably appear to some as an act of far-seeing statesmanship.

On the other side, however, must be set, leaving India out for the moment, two considerations, neither without weight: to wit, first that the capital of the Turkish Empire was not Great Britain's to dispose of; and, second, that the offer blithely sought to accomplish, at a pen's stroke and without the privity of British public opinion, just that which Great Britain had for generations been putting forth all her ingenuity to prevent. In India the business took on yet another aspect, inasmuch as Russia has ever shown herself the relentless foe of Islam, as well as a standing menace to Indian security.

In face of such rumours, whether well or ill founded, it was not surprising that India should become bewildered, disheartened, lukewarm rather than not in a cause of which the true issues were more than ever hidden from her.

The Indian Government took prompt measures to allay anxiety, on the old familiar lines. Pledges were given, ample and satisfying, in so far as pledges, as such, can satisfy. The integrity of the Turkish Empire was not in danger, the sovereignty of the Sultan in no way threatened, nor ever had been. The "rich lands of Thrace," with the holy city of Adrianople, would still be Turkish, as of yore—nothing was left unsaid which could tend to reassure Muslim opinion in India and restore in the fullest measure that spirit of confidence which had been so miraculously contrived in the first instance.

But the pledges, ample and satisfying, came from the lips of the then Viceroy, Lord Hardinge, and it was Lord Hardinge, according to rumour (which was by this time rumour no longer, but sober and ascertained fact), who had in his own person borne a principal part in the negotiations for the Constantinople bargain. These divergent truths, with their unity of origin and fundamental disunity of purport, becoming known and weighed and compared together, could not fail to produce an unpleasant impression. Not only must they needs tend to destroy confidence in the ample and satisfying pledges, but also to raise certain vague, far-reaching and most undesirable doubts as to British good faith in general.

There was a time, and not long ago, when the word of an Englishman (and surely the word of England should be the same) was a sacred bond. It is a million pities that such ideas should be now things of the past—that a mess of pottage, so unaccountably savoury, should be deemed worth the sacrifice of a birthright so precious.

Such were the doubts engendered in India by the diplomatic manipulations of Lord Hardinge—manipulations conceived on the Machiavellian scale, but lacking the *finesse* of the master. British diplomacy is not built on the lines of Machiavelli, although a long record of straight dealing may have given that impression to minds naturally tortuous. British diplomacy could not survive the acid test. Machiavelli would never have allowed himself to be "caught out" so early. The rest is history. India's doubts have been more than justified. The ample and satisfying pledges, though confirmed by a British Prime Minister in the House of Commons, have not been kept.

There has never been any intention to keep them—that is pretty generally admitted now—and the hysterical Crusading talk of responsible British politicians has given additional proof, if such were necessary, that religion was to be exploited from motives of policy, and that the war in the Near East was to be made a war of religion. The Arab-Jew question in Palestine helps to prove that pledges given by the diplomats in their utmost need are honoured more in the breach than otherwise.

Current political talk runs openly on these lines to-day. Every utterance of every politician, which has for its topic the blessed principle of the Rights of Minorities, Self-Determination, Realization of Aspirations, or any other of Dr. Wilson's kindly conceived beatitudes, as applied to the Near East, is to be approached from the point of view of Religion, and to have Religion for its object, ostensible at least.

Interference on religious grounds, if sincere, must be impartial, and not confined to Christian communities in Muslim States. If the British Government were sincere in its sympathy for religious disability, where found, would it not be justified in interfering on behalf of the 40,000,000 Muslims of Java, on the ground that they are co-religionists of a vast number of British subjects, besides being subjects of the Caliphate? But British government is Christian government, and there has been no interference.

CHAPTER V

AFTER THE TREATY OF SÈVRES

THE Treaty of Sèvres has opened the eyes of the Muslim, if hitherto closed. He had found that all the principles of democracy, the boast of the English nation, were only, after all, the privilege of the English people, and were not for him. During the war he was told that the participation of Great Britain in the world-conflict was for the democratisation of the world—in the words of Dr. Wilson, "to make the world safe for democracy." At a crisis of grave and imminent peril he heard the Premier declare in a speech at Glasgow that the Government had been a libel on the name and teaching of Jesus, and that they would make amends if they won the war, and see to it that every land be free and open to every people. The words are still ringing in the ears of Muslims, for the principle of making every land accessible to every man is a Qur-ánic principle. He was rejoiced to hear Mr. Balfour saying, in his thanksgiving speech after the Armistice, that if God was pleased to give victory to the British nation, it was not on account of their prowess or strategy, but because the principles of government for which they fought were the principles of democracy, that is, of justice and fair dealing between nation and nation as between man and man. In short, the war was declared to be a war between democracy and military despotism, which, from the Qur-ánic point of view, was a war between Islam and infidelity, and the Muslim's duty was naturally to support the former. He had his own misgivings, too, lest the war should prove, after all, a fight between Christianity and Islam. His doubts became strengthened when the secret treaty between Russia and England, as to the handing over of Constantinople to the former, became disclosed. He wanted a definite assurance that the result of the war would not affect the integrity of the power and suzerainty of the Sultan as *Khalifa-tul-Muslamin.* The assurance was given, and he was satisfied.

The war ended, and even before the peace was concluded the cat emerged from the bag. The deplorable event of Amritsar and impolitic support of the methods adopted in the Punjab in those days, forthcoming from certain quarters in England, suggested not merely that the

Indian estimation of England was incorrect, but that that nation was capable of acts such as are recorded of Hallaku and Ghanges of the Middle Ages. The comparison came from a President of the All-India Muslim League when he spoke of the Amritsar massacre in his presidential speech in December 1919. Then came the peace of Sèvres, and the Muslims found all the pledges of the Government broken. Leaving aside the most impolitic remarks in which Messrs. Asquith and Lloyd George saw fit to indulge from time to time, and which tended more and more to make the war appear a war between Christendom and Islam, the very mode of settlement of the Turkish territories made clear the religious character thus imposed on the struggle. Christian minorities under Turkish rule have become mere pretexts for dismemberment or intervention from without. New *régimes* in Smyrna and Adrianople are proposed, with supervisory powers vested in the League of Nations, and again Christian minorities supply the reason. No such proposals would have been possible but for the war, and the Muslim is forced to the conclusion that the war was for Christianity—to the detriment of Islam. No interest, be it noted, was evinced in the Muslim minorities in the Balkan States when a settlement was made with them.

I have already pointed out that from a Muslim point of view a government has to represent and safeguard the interest of the governed. The gain and loss of the government are the gain and loss of the governed. If the war has indeed been won, it has been won by the British Government for the benefit of those under the British government, including the Muslim, who is, in fact, in a majority. If the Christian British subjects can demand interference from the British Government in the interest of their co-religionists in other countries, the right to make a similar demand attaches with fourfold force to the Muslim British subjects. Their number is more than four times that of the Christian. If Greeks and Armenians are the co-religionists of the smaller community under British rule, the Turks are co-religionists of the greater. But the question of Turkey has yet another aspect. The Turkish Sultan is the universally accepted Caliph of the Muslims, and the Caliphate in Islam, is, as I will explain, of vital importance to Muslims. If the plea of Christian interests being in danger has, from time to time, justified British interference in the government of other countries, then the question of the Caliphate surely justifies the Muslims of India in requesting their government (which is the British government) to interfere in the matter on their behalf. A government, in the Muslim view, can only justify its existence by giving heed to the voice of the governed, as I have shown in the first chapter. Suppose there had been no war, and the Caliphate was in danger from some other quarter: the Muslim would have deemed it his legitimate right to compel the government to interfere and protect the Caliphate. But what an irony of fate and faith! The very body to which the Muslim in India looks for help turns out to be his adversary.

The Greco-Turk War served only to confirm this opinion. While the Indian Muslim is sending financial help to the Angora Government, he finds the British Government facilitating the same in favour of his enemies—the Greeks. To quote *The Times*, February 5th:

> We have the testimony of Lord Northcliffe that the permission given by the Government to Greece to raise a loan of £15,000,000 in this country has been deeply resented by Indian Muslims. The Government's blunder has been accentuated by the more recent proposal to permit Greece to obtain credits under the Trade Facilities Act with a British guarantee. When a country is at war, any form of financial help it may receive is in effect help in the waging of war.

What a lack of imagination! Could such

counter moves on the political chessboard by the ruled and the rulers create any good will between the two ?

Deputation after deputation came, but all the representations made, and repeated, fell on deaf ears. The Muslim was in a dilemma when events began, or seemed to begin, to take this turn. He could not openly side with sedition, neither could he conspire secretly against his rulers, this being contrary to the teachings of his religion. He felt that it would not be possible to live under such a government and remain loyal to it. Religion, however, came to his help. *Hijrat*—emigration from the country—was a convenient remedy recommended by Islam to meet such contingencies, and the learned in religion gave their verdict for *Hijrat*.

Does it not speak highly for the peaceful teachings of Islam ? Anarchism was not unknown to the Muslim as a means to achieve a political end. His neighbours in the country had resorted to it, when the Bengal partition was distasteful to them ; but Islam came in his way ; Islam permitted no such course. He preferred *Hijrat*, and thereby showed to the utmost his dissatisfaction with the rule, against which, as a true Muslim, he would not rebel. Thousands of Muslims sold their valuable property for paltry sums under the pressure of the moment and left the country with their families for Afghanistan. This went on for a few months, but new developments in the diplomatic relations between the British Government and Afghanistan affected the movement, and it had to be given up. Many of the *Muhajirn* (emigrants) came back from Afghanistan penniless and houseless. They saw their salvation only in making joint efforts with their fellow-countrymen to get their grievances redressed.

Is it, then, surprising that the Muslim should rally to the flag of Mahatma Gandhi and deem himself justified in furthering the cause of civil disobedience ? The Muslim is not unaware of the theory on which all taxation is based. To him it is a fee for the services of protecting the life, property and other interests of the taxpayer. He levies a tax in like manner on non-Muslims in Muslim territories, which Christian propagandists have called a "poll-tax on infidels." A Muslim under Muslim rule is subject to conscription for the defence of the country; he has to pay also a special tax for the poor, and various other taxes. A non-Muslim under Muslim rule has been freed by the law from all such taxes and from military service, and he has simply to pay a tax for the protection of his property and other interests. This is what has been branded as the poll-tax. To put it shortly, the Muslim has been taught by his religion the theory of taxation, which can only be levied validly if used to further and protect the interests of those who are called upon to pay; and if the Caliphate is an interest of supreme importance to him, can he be willing to pay taxes if the body which receives them not only does not protect the Caliphate, but, in ignorance, does many things which imperil it? I say in ignorance, because the Cabinet represents a nation which is not interested in injuring its fellow-subjects. This much I can affirm, from my own knowledge of the nation.

Mr. Gandhi has gone to jail, and may die there; but his principles, as far as I can judge, are taking deep root in the minds of the people, who have been forced to the belief that whatever they pay in the form of taxes and rates is not being rightly used. There is no vital necessity for the Muslim to follow Mr. Gandhi. It would not be a difficult matter to wean him from this new allegiance, but he cannot go against his own religion. His conception of government is quite clear to him; an alien rule is no grievance to him, so long as that rule adheres to the following principles of Omar on the administration of the government:

My Brothers, I owe you several duties and you have

several rights over me. One of them is that you should see that I do not misuse the revenues; another that I may not adopt wrong measures in the assessment of the revenue; that I should increase your salaries; protect the frontiers; and that I should not involve you in any unnecessary dangers. Whenever I err, you have the right to stop and take me to task.

Who can deny the wisdom or the truth in these words of Omar? Personal religion should not be allowed to sway the judgment of those who hold the reins and responsibilities of government in their hands. They are the representatives not of the King of England, but of a monarch who rules the destinies of the adherents of many religions, among whom Muslims preponderate in number. He is defender of the faith, but the word "faith" must not be taken in the narrow sense of four centuries ago. It should connote Islam, Hinduism, Buddhism, Christianity, Judaism, Sikhism, Parsiism, and the rest. It is a pity that to placate certain powerful religious interests in this country, whose support is of vital importance in party government, the Cabinet should become a helpless instrument in their hands.

Unfortunately, the last thirty years have seen Islam being constantly weakened by the Christian Powers, and the Muslims in India have reason to suspect the presence of a British hand in this game against Islam. Prior to the war the process was one affecting the geographical boundaries of these countries, but the war itself could never have aroused such an upheaval of unrest in all Muslim lands if the foolish policy of certain statesmen, egged on by religious bigotry in this country, had not led Muslims to believe that the war was, after all, a war between Islam and Christianity.

CHAPTER VI

INCENDIARISM AND THE GOVERNMENT'S DRASTIC MEASURES

To dub the political worker in India a firebrand may, or may not, serve a useful purpose; but it will certainly not be of any assistance to those who are seeking to understand the real character of the people with whom they have to deal.

Civil disobedience in India is, no doubt, fraught with many dangers, and the sooner it comes to an end the better, for the sake both of the ruler and the ruled. But the measures adopted by the British Government will prove futile in the long run. Unfortunately, no true and proper information of the state of things in India is ever laid before the people here. Not even the hundredth part of the gravity of the situation there has, as yet, been appreciated. What I read in the Indian vernacular newspapers simply strengthens my conviction that whatever appears in the English daily papers is written in ignorance, due to lack of adequate means for obtaining proper means of information. It is never a good policy to suppress the truth. Mahatma Ghandi's imprisonment may seem to improve matters to those who do not like to face realities and those who believe in opportunism.

Of late, much has been made in the Press of certain co-called " drastic measures " which are being adopted. Every new arrest, especially if the person arrested be a person of importance in India, is hailed with approval and regarded as a " step in the right direction." From the same point of view Mr. Montagu's dismissal from the India Office is held to be fully justified; but it is not a paying policy to permit the spirit of party politics to hamper or defeat those who are dealing with the problem of India's affairs in all honesty of purpose, and with the wide vision of true statesmanship. I do not believe that any Englishman would lend his countenance to harsh measures that can serve no good purpose. It is the practical utility of any proposed measure which should more than anything else guide the conduct of a statesman. Those who lay stress on a " strong rule " merely show ignorance of the psychology of the people with whom they have to deal.

My attention has been called to a statement

in the editorial columns of the *Pall Mall Gazette* (April 25, 1922), which, though it may well command ready credence from those who are content with hoping for the best, is yet so utterly at variance with the actual position of affairs that it becomes my plain duty, so far as in me lies, to open the eyes of the people of this country and convince them that they are, in very deed, living in a fools' paradise.

The statement is as follows:

> The news from India shows that Mr. Montagu's departure from office has had a wholesome effect upon the general tone and condition.
>
> The restoration of a real spirit of government and the decision to give authority the support so long withheld from it have had immediate results, and the disorderly element has been cooled by the imprisonment of Gandhi and other leaders.
>
> The greatest crime against a country like India is to give the impression that its rulers are timid in the face of incendiarism. It is a wrong that will not be repeated, we trust, in this generation.

It is possible that this "greatest crime against a country like India" may "not be repeated, at least in this generation," but whether because of the "restoration of the spirit of real government" or of some new and wholly startling change in the "real government" itself, the next few years must now decide.

Apart, however, from its air of complacent optimism, the *Pall Mall Gazette*'s facts are fundamentally in error. The imprisonment of Mr. Gandhi has brought calm instead of unrest, order out of disorder, because the gospel that he preached—the spirit raised up by him—has, it is argued, been cowed by a show of force. Here is complacency indeed —but how little is it justified!

The calm is there, but, so far from giving promise of fair weather after storm, it is in itself a storm sign so strange that the recorder of political meteorology would be hard put to it to find a parallel.

Let me quote the following public appeal made by Mr. S. Srinavasa Iyengar, lately Advocate-General of Madras, published in the *Rangoon Mail*, March 24, 1922; and let me point out by way of preface that its author is no firebrand, no agitator or extremist, but a responsible person with a "stake in the country," a professional man, one who has held high office under the Government and fairly represents the actual trend to-day of "Moderate" public opinion in India:

> This is the hour of our supreme trial. But it is our duty, if we are sincere in our devotion to Mahatma Gandhi and to his radiant gospel of truth and work, of strenuous peace and cheerful renunciation, to follow his latest advice in its spirit and to its very letter. I

hope that we will all realize, whatever our political views or our temperamental differences may be, that to us Indians, whether Hindus, Muhammadans, Sikhs or Christians, Brahmins, non-Brahmins or non-caste Hindus, *he is the very greatest of our countrymen, that in him there is neither hate nor bitterness, neither weakness nor arrogance, and that he is to us the perfect embodiment of all that is highest, noblest and holiest in our great and immemorial culture.* I hope you will also realize that to millions of our countrymen he has brought a strange happiness in an era of great economic and moral depression, and he has given us a message which will last as long as the world lasts. Have we not all felt in our hearts, whatever our political, religious or social differences may be, and however much our westernized minds might rebel against the idea, that *his place is amongst the great founders of the world-religions, along with Krishna, Buddha, Christ or Muhammad,* and that he has purified, strengthened and elevated us, and made us a manlier and more united people, more than anyone else has done since the dawn of Indian history ?

We must hereafter regard the 10th of March, the day of his arrest, *as a historic day,* the commencement of a new era of Indian nationalism. We must, in memory of that day, enter into a solemn league and covenant, forthwith, before God, pledging ourselves to full Swadeshi, absolute non-violence, loving social service, and the most perfect and determined national unity. In every town and village, men, women and children should, without any preaching of propaganda, make it a point of personal and national honour to purchase and wear and otherwise *to encourage Swadeshi that is hand-spun and hand-woven.* We must as the next article of faith abstain religiously from leasing our cocoanut-trees for tapping, and most peacefully carry on our Anti-Drink Campaign. Above all, Hindu-Muslim Unity, *that most precious of Mahatma Gandhi's gifts to us* should be maintained and increased as if he is still with us and if we are every day seeing and hearing him.

May I not hope that this hour shall find us all, *non-co-operators or co-operators, reunited, all our differences forgotten and our mutual offences forgiven? Lives there a single Indian who on account of political differences will now fail to honour Mahatma Gandhi,* let him show it in the way God and his conscience tell him to do. Neither *hartals* nor processions nor meetings, but a day of fast and prayer should be observed by us in honour of the *greatest saint of modern times,* who has so successfully worked with unexampled energy, zeal and courage for the salvation of the millions of his countrymen. Is it too much to expect that the members of our Legislative Assemblies or Councils, who have without any avail striven to do their best during the last two or three weeks, will complete their efforts by the indispensable but easy sacrifice of their seats? We must maintain at all times and in all places the peace of Gandhi inviolate and the marvellous discipline which has distinguished congressmen in these days, and in no wise or degree fallen away from the high standard and the great achievements which have so far characterized our great national movement. If we do that, I have no doubt that we shall be able to give a good account of ourselves to Mahatma Gandhi when he comes back to us.[1]

This is not "unrest" in the commonly accepted political significance of the word. You cannot deal with a man like this as you would deal with a street-corner agitator or a bomb-throwing fanatic. It signifies, on the other hand, a vast and unmistakably national movement—coherent and ordered; comprehending all classes of the community, literate and illiterate, gentle and simple; inspired by a living devotion to a lofty ideal both in

[1] The italics are mine.

aim and conduct, which finds its outward symbol in a leader, reverenced by millions as of the fellowship of the prophets, whose watchword is selflessness.

The Indian mind is, as a rule, less materialistic than the European. When stirred by religion, the Indian becomes indifferent to pains and pleasures. He whose object or ideal is but coexistent with his own activities or his life may perhaps respond to coercive measures; but he whose vision passes beyond this transitory life will not be greatly perturbed by its troubles and trials. Dr. Satyapal, a famous Amritsar leader, and a firm believer, like other Hindus, in the transmigration of souls, when threatened with death under the Punjab martial law of 1919, was reported to have said to the officer from whom the threat came that he would rather have death than a miserable life such as he was eking out under the Government's tyranny, in punishment for the sins he might have committed in a previous existence. To him the present administration appeared to be nothing less than a scourge from God to punish the wrongs of that previous life. If death, or any other hardship, is believed to be a necessary sequel of certain past misdeeds, which being thus expiated, bliss will follow in the life to come, it will more be welcomed than shuddered at, more especially when men's minds are tense and highly wrought. It is not the government of the country that the Indians resent, but they seek salvation from tyranny and injustice, which, they think, are materialized in the present method of rule. They have no grudge against the King. They love and respect him. It is the administration given to them on his behalf that, they say, they detest. They saw to the personal safety of the Prince of Wales, but, inasmuch as the invitation to him to visit India came from the administration, they would not co-operate with it.

It would almost seem that this campaign has been started with motives higher than those of mere earthly gain; that religious fervour and devotion to a sublime ideal are of its very essence. Call it frenzy or fanaticism, what you will—it hardly affects the issue: a martyr-like devotion inspires the whole movement; men deem themselves responding to the call of a most sacred duty, which they must perform at any cost. With calmness and level judgment they face all the hardships in their way; a halo of dignity is around them when they stand in court to take their trial. They refuse to speak a word in their own defence, because they regard the whole judicial procedure as a farce; they hear their judgment pronounced with smiles and go to jail composedly and serenely, with a word of advice to them that come after to do as they themselves have done, but without violence of any kind. Men of wealth and social standing, of education and discernment, Hindus and Muslims, go to prison gladly, with those of the humbler sort—to the astonishment of Lord Reading—because, they say, *in prison they know what to expect, but at large, in a so-called free land, they no longer know it. They call it worse than slavery.* These, to the best of my recollection, are the words of the son of the famous Moderate, the Pandit Madan Mohan Malviya, when on trial. When in jail, and sometimes even before the trial begins, they are offered release on the condition that they refrain from any repetition of the conduct with which they have been charged, but they invariably refuse.

The statement[1] of such a one when accused is worthy of study; in it you will find no nonsense, but a well-judged and well-balanced marshalling of facts, exposing that which they style "misrule," "tyranny" and "oppression." You charge and punish them for one or two such statements made outside; but the statements which, as accused persons, they are entitled to give, and for which they cannot be punished, and which may be pub-

[1] See Appendix IV, Statement of Mahatma Gandhi.

lished and repeated in the public Press without entailing any penalty, disclose allegations which, if stated elsewhere, would make the crime under the present judiciary in India ten times graver. There is another circumstance attendant on certain of these cases, which completely defeats the object of the trial. When a person is accused and brought to the bar for a seditious statement, the court becomes crowded with thousands of men repeating the identical statement and expressing their willingness to be tried for it. I myself witnessed such a scene in Rangoon (Burma) in 1921. Sometimes, also, mass meetings of tens of thousands of people are convened in different towns, and the very statement for which some man is then standing his trial is put into the form of a resolution and passed unanimously. This occurred in the trial of the Ali Brothers. You cannot send thousands of people to jail. Moreover, the relations of the convict receive, instead of messages of condolence from their friends, cables of congratulation. Mass meetings are held, and congratulatory resolutions passed and conveyed to the prisoner and his relatives. Ballads and songs praising jail and imprisonment for one's country's salvation are composed and circulated ; and you will find quite young children humming them in the streets. If jail-life has become an ideal life, and a certificate of martyrdom and leadership, as one of the Calcutta (English) papers remarked in 1920 concerning Dr. Kitchlew, Ph.D., of Amritsar, can imprisonment or any other treatment, however hard, produce the desired result?

The only possible good that can arise from such trials is the removal of certain political workers from the scene of their activities for the period of their imprisonment. But the positive harm that ensues is infinitely greater. First, there is no lack of persons willing and eager to follow Gandhi and the Ali Brothers to prison, and each trial brings forth other workers in the field; and, secondly, the so-called "firebrands" are not considered "firebrands" by their fellow-countrymen. Even those who differ from them in opinion respect them for their sincerity, selflessness and piety. These "firebrands" may err in judgment, but no one for one moment doubts their honesty of purpose. They are, on the contrary, revered as men of saintly character.

The presiding judge, Mr. Broomfield, was constrained to make the following observation when he addressed Mahatma Gandhi before pronouncing judgment:

> The law is no respecter of persons. Nevertheless, it will be impossible to ignore the fact that you are in a

different category from any person I have ever tried or am ever likely to have to try. Also, it would be impossible to ignore the fact that in *the eyes of millions of your countrymen you are a great patriot and a great leader, or that even those who differ from you in politics look up to you as a man of high ideals and leading a noble and even a saintly life.* I have to deal with you in one character only. It is not my duty, and I do not presume, to judge or criticize you in any other character. It is my duty to judge you as a man subject to the law, who by his own admission has broken the law and committed what to an ordinary man must appear to be a grave offence against the State.

The judge, in passing sentence, said: "If the course of events in India should make it possible for the Government to reduce the period and release you, no one will be better pleased than I."

The Advocate-General of Madras, from whom I have quoted elsewhere, does but voice the feeling in the hearts of millions of Indians when he speaks of Mahatma Gandhi. With all due respect to the Mahatma, my surprise, however, knows no bounds when I see a section of the Muslims hailing him as a prophet; because it is sin for us Muslims to accept any person as a prophet after the Holy Prophet Muhammad. Most of the political workers in India are gentlemen of high repute; their actions and antecedents have always been aboveboard; they have joined the movement, not from any sordid motives, but for the cause itself, which they, and especially the Muslims among them, believe to be of a character so high, noble and religious as to demand any sacrifice, however great. They have given up their lucrative pursuits; they lead rigid and abstemious lives. They have renounced affluence and live the life of a beggar. This I can vouch for from my own personal knowledge of men like C. R. Das, Motilal, Jawahirtal Nehrus, Swami Durshnanand, Chawdri Rambhaj Dutt, Dr. Santanum, Professor Vaswani, L. Duni Chand, Lalla Lajpat Rai, Sirjut Jitandralal Banerjie, Sirjut Shyam Sunder Chakravarty, Sirdar Sirdool Singh, the Ali Brothers, Hakim Ajmal Khan, Dr. Ansari, Maulana Abdul Bari, Maulana Abul Kalam, Khwaja Abdul Majid, Dr. Mohammed Alam, Zafarali Khân, Hasrat Mohâni, M. Azad Sybhani, Yacoob Hasan, Aga Mohammed Sufdar Khan, Maulvi Abdul Qadir and many others, both Hindus and Muslims. Such men cannot be kept back from their purpose; hardship and persecution have no terrors for them. Rather do they court suffering, and welcome it when it comes to them, because selfish or materialistic gain is no part of their motive.

I have ventured thus briefly to indicate the moral calibre of these men, so that the people here in England may be able to appreciate the psychology of the situation before launching any measure of coercion.

It will now be obvious that the measures adopted by the Indian Government, perhaps at the dictation of the Home Government—drastic, firm, or strong, describe them by any epithet that pleases you—will never, in my humble opinion, act as a deterrent. They have already failed in their object. A man may disagree with you on practically every point, but if by your sincerity and selflessness you command his respect, any persecution that you may be called upon to suffer on account of these very things upon which you differ, will not only serve to accentuate his sympathy, but may probably also make him your defender, and perhaps turn him against your persecutors. It is precisely this psychological process that I see at work in India to-day. Many of those who at one time differed with Gandhi and the Ali Brothers are now, as a result of these trials, taking sides with them.[1]

[1] Speaking of the arrest and imprisonment of the leaders of repute, Pandit Madan Mohan Malviya, one of the well-known leaders of the Moderate party and a gentleman of very high repute in India, observed that the only offence for which they had been shut up in jail lay in their opposition to the Government at a time when the latter was waging a war against their fundamental rights of citizenship. He wanted to probe, he went on, the depth of Indian feeling and sentiment

There are many among the "Moderates" who do not approve the Government's action. They have tried to turn those in authority from this policy of repression. What occurred in the Legislative Assembly when the Government was defeated on the question of the Military Estimates only strengthens me in my view. Non-co-operation has, so far as the importation of English goods is concerned, received fresh impetus from the imprisonment of the Mahatma. The Bombay Cloth Merchants' Association, in honour of the event, passed a fresh resolution against the importation of foreign goods, providing penalties for those who should infringe it; and it is barely two years since this same association was among the most determined enemies of the non-co-operation movement.

Those of the Indian Civil Service who, during their stay in India, have cared to go beyond official red-tape, and have studied the Indian mind to help them in their official work, will not fail to endorse what I have said. You should consult Roose Keppels, Thorburns, Wilsons, Cunninghams, if you would understand the Indian minds in the

and to know whether they were yet prepared to overhaul a system of administration which knew no better use for the best sons of the land than to let them rot in jails.—*The Vakel Amritsar*, April 14, 1922.

North, rather than be guided by the opportunists who take fancy for facts, before you formulate any policy; and in this connection it would not be out of place if I quote from the letter of Sir Hamilton Grant, the Chief Commissioner of the Frontier Province, which recently appeared in the columns of *The Times*:

> The chronic British apathy towards Indian affairs has lately given place to an almost hysterical interest, and on all sides one hears discussion, sometimes intelligent, more often ill-informed, of the situation in that distressful country. Criticism of the policy of His Majesty's Government and of the Government of India is rife, and all manner of remedies, generally drastic, often fantastic, are suggested. But in all this talk there is one thing deplorably lacking, and that is the old spirit of good will towards India and her varied peoples. . . .
>
> There are two things that it would be well that people in England should realize; first, that it is quite untrue that the only thing the Oriental understands is force; and second, that there is much in the character of the peoples of India that deserves respect, affection and often admiration. Generally speaking, the Oriental fears less than the European. For he is a fatalist, and often a very brave man. The psychology of the view that machine-guns are the panacea for Indian unrest is as false as the Prussian doctrine of "frightfulness." Even an unmartial Bengali can walk steadily to the gallows for a cause in which he believes. As to character, those who have served among Pathans, Sikhs, Dogras, Punjabi Moslems, and the many kindly peoples of the plains and hills of Northern India will agree that for personal courage, self-sacrificing devotion and hospitality it would be difficult to find their equal. It would be well that this

should be remembered, and that there should be no wholesale condemnation of India because of the dangerous activities of a comparatively few agitators. Law and order must, of course, be ruthlessly maintained, but we should deplore rather than welcome the necessity for drastic measures against peoples by nature so fine and lovable.

One word more. Many of the young men who have gone out to India in the last few years have had most pernicious and distorted views of the way in which Indians should be treated; and—I say it with shame—these views are usually shared by their womenfolk. The exemplary punishment of flagrant cases of maltreatment, though necessary, does not cure the evil. We must have public opinion strongly against all hectoring and bullying and wanton discourtesy. For such things are not only cowardly and disgraceful in themselves, but they also do our position in India infinite harm, and make the re-establishment of good will impossible. Good will may be vague and intangible, but it is none the less a great force, and we can regive and regain it, not by concession to agitation or pandering to political schemers, but by kindliness in thought, word and deed, by geniality and good manners to people who are themselves the best-mannered in the world.

CHAPTER VII

THE CALIPHATE

I NEED not emphasize here the importance and need of the Caliphate in Islam. The Muslim anxiety for the security of this institution, which has become identified with the Turkish Empire for the last five hundred years, has always manifested itself in the most emphatic manner on every occasion in which Turkey has been in trouble, since the days of the Crimean War. The present unrest in Muslim India is to be explained in like manner. The eyes of English statesmen have at last become opened to it. The wisest statecraft admits, though with some reluctance, that the satisfactory settlement of this question constitutes the sole guarantee of safety and peace for British rule in India. Leaving apart Muslim India, the country cannot remain free from troubles coming from the border tribes unless the matter is settled to the satisfaction of the Muslims of the world. The Home Government has realized the situation, but the suggested method of adjustment shows ignorance, if not a want of good intention.

I do not propose to lay down any policy or dictate any terms on behalf of the Muslims. I simply put forward here the bare facts of the case to help the Government and the people of Great Britain to pursue a course befitting a Government whose intent it is to govern for the benefit of a community which outnumbers all other communities under British rule. It will not do good to trifle with a matter of serious import, like the Caliphate.

THE ORIGIN OF THE CALIPHATE

Allah has promised to those of you who believe and do good that He will most certainly make them Khalifas (successors or rulers) in the land as He made those to be rulers who were before them, and that He will most certainly establish for them their religion which He has chosen for them, and *that He will most certainly, after their fear, give them security in exchange;* they shall serve Me, not associating aught with Me, and whoever is ungrateful after this, those it is who are the transgressors (xxiv. 55).

The above quotation from the Holy Qur-án stands as the basis of the Muslim Caliphate. The verse is generally known among Muslims as the verse speaking of the Caliphate. The word "Istakhlafa," which occurs in the original text, means "He made him a ruler." Though the meaning here is quite clear, yet I quote a few commentators to show that this meaning has always been universally accepted. Baizawi: "He will make them Khalifa in the *land*, i.e. He will make them rulers having control in the *land*, as kings control their kingdom." Kasháf: "He will make them inherit the *land*, and make them Khalifas in it." Ruh-ul-Ma'ani: "He will make them rulers acting in the *land* as they please, like kings act in their kingdoms as they please." Ibn-i-Kasir: "He will make the followers of the Prophet rulers of the *land*, i.e. the leaders of the people and controlling their affairs." Ibn-i-Jabir; "Allah will make them inherit the *land* from the non-Muslims of Arabia and Ajum, so that He will make them its king and chief man." The verse also speaks of "Al-ard"—the land—with which the Caliphs shall have a direct connection as its rulers. Here, again, I quote various commentators to show what the word "Al-ard" in the verse—the land—signifies. Baizawi: "The messenger of God—may peace and the blessing of God be upon him—and his companions had lived at Mecca for ten years; fearing then, they fled to Medina and lived in arms morning and evening *until God fulfilled His promise* and made them masters of the whole of Arabia. In this there is an argument of the truth of prophethood on account of the news of the unseen and of the Caliphate." Gharaib-ul-Qur-án: "So God fulfilled His promise and made them masters of the Jazairat-ul-Arab, and they also inherited the kingdom of Kisera, and their treasures." Kasháf: "So God fulfilled His promise and made them masters of the Jazairat-ul-Arab." Fath-ul-Bayan: "Ibn-i-Arabi says: It means Arabia and countries other than Arabia, and this is the correct view." Ruh-ul-Ma'ani: "And by Al-Arab is meant, as had been said, Jazairat-ul-Arab." Ibn-i-Kasir: "This is a promise from God to His messenger, peace be on him, that He will make his followers Khalifas in the earth. So the Holy Prophet did not die until God brought in subjugation to him Mecca and Khaibar, and the whole of Jazairat-ul-Arab, and the land of Yamen in its entirety, and he took taxes from the Magi of Hajer and from some quarters of Syria."

Thus it is clear that all the commentators have taken this verse as the basis of the Caliphate, and read in it a promise for the kingship of the whole of the Jazairat-ul-Arab, as the nucleus around which was to grow the vast Muslim Empire. The promise of the Caliphate has always been understood by the best authorities as amounting to a promise for the establishment of an empire, of which Arabia was always to be an essential part. Without an independent empire free from outside interference, without rule over Arabia, the Caliphate is meaningless. Arabia was the central kingdom "in the Caliphate," in the sense that while other portions of the empire might change, Arabia could not. There might be other Muslim empires in the world, but the Caliphate rested with that empire of which Arabia was part, inasmuch as the Caliphate meant a successorship to the Holy Prophet, and the Jazairat-ul-Arab being the kingdom which the Prophet left at his death, had become an essential part of the Caliphate. If a Caliph loses Arabia he can no longer be called a successor of the Holy Prophet. The very word Caliph makes it obligatory that he shall have authority over Arabia, with other territory to maintain his authority and to serve the other needs of the Caliphate.[1] Other Muslim empires have existed, sometimes very great ones, but they have never been recognized as the Caliphate, because they did not rule over Arabia. On the other hand, such empires have recognized the Caliphate, as I will show later on.

For the last thirteen hundred years Arabia

[1] See Chapter VIII.

has always remained under the Caliph. The first four Caliphs ruled from Medina, and though Muawiya had his seat of government at Damascus, Arabia was still a province of the empire, and so it remained under all the Umayyad kings. Under the Abbasids, the capital of the Caliphate was Baghdad, but the governors of the different districts of Arabia were appointed by the Caliph. From the Abbasids, the Caliphate passed to the Turks, with some intervals of the Fatamites, and since then Arabia has been under the control of Turkey, though some of the districts, through the intrigue of the Western Powers, have revolted.

Islam requires the maintenance of a strong Muslim empire, with authority extending over the whole of Arabia, as a religious necessity. The Prophet himself was a king, as well as a teacher, and so must be his Caliph. The Muslims find a promise of such an empire in the Holy Qur-án. They have seen it for the last thirteen hundred years, and any attempt on the part of the English Government to weaken, dismember or efface such government would be taken as tantamount to an attempt to weaken Islam and put the words of the Qur-án to nought. The words of the Qur-án run thus:

And that He will most certainly establish for them

their religion, which He has chosen for them, and that He will most certainly after this fear give them security in exchange.

These words are the concluding portions of the verse speaking of the Caliphate. The prophetical promise makes it clear that temporal rule of the Muslims in this case is necessary for the firm establishment of their religion and for their own security. "Islam was a true religion, even when the Holy Prophet could not freely preach its principles, when he was persecuted severely by his enemies; but it was not then firmly established, nor were the Muslims then secure. And if the political power of Islam is again brought to nought by Christian Europe, it would not affect the truth of the religion of Islam at all; it would only mean that a blow is dealt to the firm establishment of Islam in the world, and that the real security of the Muslims has been taken away. It is this that every Muslim heart feels. That feeling is not some feeble awakening to impending danger; it is the Muslim's strongest faith and surest belief, based on the clear words of the Holy Qur-án, *that those who seek to weaken the Muslim Caliphate are really aiming at weakening Islam*, and that the Muslims will be no more secure in the world, all the so-called religious liberty notwithstanding. The Caliphate is therefore a necessity for the Muslims, not only because it is rendered necessary by the words of the Holy Qur-án, but also because the Word of God has told the Muslims that the weakening of the Caliphate means the weakening of the religion of Islam, and is a clear sign of insecurity for the Muslims in the world. And what the Word of God has pointed out so clearly is now seen by every Muslim eye as clearly mirrored forth in the trend of events."

The above I quote from the writings of an Indian Muslim theologian renowned throughout the Muslim world. I mean his Holiness Hazarat Maulvi Mohamed Ali, the President of the Anjuman Ishat-e-Islam, Lahore, who, like myself, has always refrained most scrupulously from dabbling with politics. He has simply mirrored Muslim minds in general; because I read the same in the writings of other Muslim theologians on the question. With all their petty differences and sectarianism, the whole Muslim world, be it Shiat or Sunniyat, has got but one word on the Caliphate. The Caliphate in Islam means the temporal and religious leadership of the Muslims, and should not be confused with the Papacy in Christendom. It means an independent empire, with Arabia as its dependency, with power enough to maintain safety and security in Arabia and keep the religious seat of Islam immune from internal and external dangers. The Caliph in past days had to protect and accord his help when needed to other Muslim kingdoms. The same author says: "The trend of events in the world's history has only proved the truth of the words of the Holy Qur-án, for the weakening of the Caliphate is the last blow, a blow at the centre of Islam, which the hostile forces could deal. Kingdom after kingdom has fallen down, away from the centre, and when there remains no vestige of another independent Muslim kingdom in the world, Turkey, which has been identified by the Muslims with their Caliphate for centuries, is threatened with the same fate. The Caliphate, or the *Divinely promised empire of Islam,* is the last of the great Muslim rule, which it is sought to sweep off. These lamentable facts only make the truth of the Qur-ánic words shine the more clearly, *and with the blow to the Caliphate no Muslim can feel himself secure, if he believes in the truth of the Qur-ánic words.*"

Mark the words which I have italicized, and the force of them becomes tenfold when I consider it as coming from one with the quiet temperament of his holiness, who in his whole life has never once taken part in the political activity of Islam. Like him, the whole priestly class of Muslim India has always remained aloof from Government affairs, but to-day they are the foremost in politics. People in England can easily imagine the influence which such a class is able to exercise on the laity in any country. The Muslims are a hundred times more touchy in religious matters than the adherents of any other religion; and consequently the situation becomes intensified by the question of the Caliphate. The reader of these pages has simply to look at the matter from the angle of an Indian Muslim, and he will readily understand both the gravity of the occasion and the justness of the Muslim cause.

For the last hundred and fifty years the Muslim has rendered faithful allegiance to Britain's rule in India, believing in her strong sense of justice and in her policy of neutrality in matters religious. The Muslim's attachment to British rule became enhanced when he saw the English nation fighting in aid of the Caliphate in the Crimean War. But he saw Tunis, Morocco, Algeria passing from Muslim to European hands. Then came the Tripolitan War, in which a new construction was put upon neutrality by the British Government when they refused to allow the Turkish forces to pass through Egypt (which was theirs under the suzerainty of the Sultan).

Till then the Muslim looked upon the British Government as the champion of the Muslims of the world on behalf of the Muslims in India, because Muslims have every right to look to the Government they are under for the furtherance of their legitimate ends throughout the whole world. Then came the Balkan War, and the suspicion that the European Chancelleries had conspired to divide the Muslim Powers among themselves began to become strengthened. The Balkan War saw a further dismemberment of the Caliphate in her own land. The present war came as the climax, and the Treaty of Sèvres proved beyond a shadow of a doubt that Islam, politically as well as from the religious standpoint, was to be swept from the surface of the earth. If the premises I have summarized in these few lines are correct, is the Muslim wrong in coming to the conclusion he has arrived at? That the Muslim sympathy is non-territorial is an established fact, seeing that it is based on the Qur-ánic teachings; that the Caliphate in all its bearings is a religious truth to a Muslim is also borne out by the Qur-án; and therefore he regards danger to the Caliphate as danger to his own religion. Could there be, therefore, any question of greater vital importance for British rule in India than this of the Caliphate?

The logic of the philo-Hellenist in England, that because Turkey threw in her lot with the enemy she should bear the consequences, does not carry much weight with Indians; for the reason that the proposed sale of Constantinople into the hands of Russia long before the war came into existence has exonerated the Turks. The Muslims in India have passed a harder ordeal in the war than ever fell to the lot of any other nation in the world. Their duty to their ruler and their duty to the Caliph were at variance, and both were religious duties; but the pledges from the highest authorities in the British Government seemed to meet the situation. They were assured of the immunity of the Caliphate; and no one can question the loyalty and faith with which the Indians fought to secure the victory. If the first efficacious check to the German onslaught in 1914 could be counted as a great factor in securing victory, the credit should go to those, the pledges to whom have now been broken. What a pity! and there can be no greater bankruptcy of statesmanship than that which the Nonconformist Premier betrayed, when he styled the conquest of Jerusalem, won through Muslim arms, as a victory of Christianity against Islam. Such parliamentary tactics, to secure support of religious bodies, which may help a party

Cabinet to remain in power, are of little consequence in comparison with what the country has lost, and is losing, in alienating India. Sheffield, Manchester, and other factory towns have already suffered. The sending of Gandhi and others to jail cannot compensate for the loss already sustained, nor can it stop the continuance of that loss. Hindus and Muslims in India, and that means the whole country, are one and decided on the question of the Caliphate and other questions. But the things are not hopeless if the Home Government will only change its course. They should pay more respect to the solemn pledges they gave to India than to the ill-considered promises they have given elsewhere.

CHAPTER VIII

THE CALIPHATE AND THE LAND OF PILGRIMAGE

HEDJAZ is the land of Muslim pilgrimage. Pilgrimage to the House of God at Mecca is one of the five pillars of Islam, and it is the cherished desire of every Muslim heart to visit the place at least once in his life. Some make many such pilgrimages to Mecca, and each year the number of pilgrims runs into many hundreds of thousands, most of whom, in addition to the act of pilgrimage, make a prolonged stay in the country. Roughly speaking, the land of Hedjaz is alive with the pilgrims for about eight months every year, that is to say, for three and a half months before and for the same period after the month of pilgrimage. They come from many countries, speaking many languages, and belong to many different civilizations—from the nomad African to the highly cultured Persian and Indian. To look to the needs, comforts, and safety of this multitude is the bounden duty of the Caliphate, for it should not be forgotten that the land of Hedjaz is the land of danger. From Jidda to Tabruk is a vast grassless desert amid naked rocks and barren mountains. No vestige of human habitation marks the way of the pilgrims between the two places. The Bedouin is the son of the desert, and feels no compunction at robbery and dacoity, even on the pilgrims; hence each pilgrim caravan (and they are thousands in number during these eight months) needs a strong police escort for its safety. Arabia is, moreover, full of tribal feuds, and the chiefs are as often as not at war with one another. Yet the land of Hedjaz must be kept free from the turbulence of these tribes. Over and above these considerations, the Wahabis of the Najd, who, in very many respects, bear a striking resemblance to the old Puritans of Christian England, are opposed to the very idea of pilgrimage to Medina, and desire nothing so much as to take possession of the Holy Tomb and hold it against the whole Muslim world. Some of them would even go so far as to destroy the sacred mausoleum and raze it to the very ground; and the history of Islam has recorded the sacrilege twice in these thirteen hundred years. A further attempt was made in the last century, when the Turks had to subdue, with the help of Muhammad Ali, the great Wahabi movement in Central Arabia. Even now the British Government pay £60,000 a year to Ibn-i-Massud and £120,000 to King Hussain for a similar object. Yemen is another thorn in the peace of the Hedjaz. The Turks made a strong effort to put down rebellion towards the end of the eighteenth century, while Yemen has become during the last fifty years and more a nest of conspiracy and foreign intrigue, and may at any time prove a menace to the safety of the land of Hedjaz.

The first duty of the Caliph is, as I have said, to maintain order in the land of Hedjaz, so that the observance of pilgrimage and other religious duties may be free from internal and external disturbance.

"And that He will most certainly establish for them their religion which He has chosen for them, and that He will most certainly, after their fear, award them security in exchange," are the Qur-ânic words, speaking the same as the verse which promises an everlasting Caliphate to the Muslims. The guardian of the Kaaba should be an independent ruler, free from outside influences, and not a puppet in the hands of others, especially if those others be non-Muslims. Hazrat Shah Wali Ullah, the great Muslim divine of the twelfth century A.H., writes the following, when speaking of the Caliphate in his famous book *Hujjatullah-el-Baleghá*: "The Caliph should be a man of matured age, with wisdom, bravery and courage. He should be independent and free. He should come from a respectable and honoured family, who could exercise influence upon others." The writer of the lines belonged to that sacred Order in Islam—*Mujaddideen*, whose words come next only to the Holy Prophet as authority in religion. The Caliph should have at his disposal force sufficiently strong to meet all reasonable contingencies. He should be powerful enough to quell all rebellion among the turbulent tribes of Arabia, and should so order affairs in Hedjaz that the pilgrims in their sojourn may feel at home and secure; more especially when they are travelling between Jidda, Medina and Tabruk. Moreover, the presence for eight months of the year of hundreds of thousands of pilgrims in Mecca and Medina demands a considerable outlay in the way of providing for the needs of the pilgrims. Every one of the thousands of caravans between Mecca and Medina needs a police escort to protect it against the Bedouin marauders. I made my pilgrimage in 1914. I travelled from Damascus to Medina by railway, and I found fully half of the compartments of the train occupied by police officers of different grades—constables, sergeants, and inspectors. The train travelled for three days and two nights through desert places, among bleak mountains and little rocky hills, with the continual risk of being derailed by robbers. At each stopping-place, when the passengers had to leave their compartments for the purchase of provisions and other necessaries, a strong police guard was essential. Trouble arose on the journey after we left Tabruk, and the Turkish constabulary was of real help to us. I found Medina full of police, as were also Mecca and Aráfátt during the days of pilgrimage. Suffice it to say that enormous outlay is necessary to maintain peace and safety of life and property even for a week. But the necessity continues for eight months out of every year, during six of which the crowd is at its greatest. Yet the pilgrims pay no tax or fee for all services rendered for their safety and comfort by the Government. The only fee I had to pay was to my guides, one in Mecca and the other in Medina, and those fees should not exceed one pound or thirty shillings in both places under the prescribed rates. The town of Medina, apart from the illumination of the Holy Shrine of the Prophet, used to be lit in those days with electric light and with many other kinds of illuminant, and guarded by hundreds of soldiers and constables. A staff of more than one hundred people remained permanently attached to each of the two shrines for various services connected with them. Imagine, I repeat, the extent of the outlay entailed upon the Government, if it is to maintain order in matters so multifarious over the thousand miles stretch—teeming with pilgrims in hundreds of thousands—between Jidda and Tabruk. I can honestly say that I found this journey of mine, even in the days of the war, a happy and comfortable one. The only inconveniences experienced by my fellow-passengers and myself were met with in those countries and on those seas which are under non-Muslim flags. All those rules and regulations of quarantine and the like appeared to the pilgrims rather in the form of impediments purposely placed in the way of the pilgrimage, than as necessary enforcements of hygienic principles. It is a fact that life and property have become unsafe in these days in the land of Hedjaz. Moreover, the pilgrims are now subjected to such tremendous additional trouble and inconvenience, that their numbers have of late become very largely decreased—as the Right Hon. Syed Amir Ali has pointed out in a recent letter to *The Times*. It is a pity that, when the victory in the Great War, secured partially through

Muslim arms, Muslim valour and sacrifice, it is Muslims who should be the chief sufferers in a matter so sacred to us as this of the Pilgrimage. In Indian judgment the blame is with Downing Street, and not with King Hussain. The Muslims, according to their conceptions of government, deem themselves entitled to see all their grievances redressed by their government to their satisfaction. Surely it would not be impossible, even now, to see the Muslim Caliphate in the hands of a monarch who, besides Arabia, rules an independent territory, with revenues enough to meet the requirements of the Hedjaz in addition to those of his own dominions. The land of Hedjaz is a land of no cultivation. As it was spoken of in the Qur-án, so it is to-day. It has no natural resources, and the Divine policy kept it so, perhaps to safeguard it against the exploiters of the world. A king of Arabia without monetary help from without cannot, other considerations apart, maintain order and organization in the Hedjaz as they have been maintained for the past thirteen hundred years. Small wonder if, with all the subsidy that King Hussain has received from the British Government, he has been compelled to levy house and other taxes in Mecca and Medina—things unknown in the annals of the Holy Places. The land of Hedjaz is a barren land and hopeless from the point of view of revenue; but to us, not only Mecca and Medina, but the whole land is a sacred shrine. Let its denizens and sojourners have peace, security from internal troubles, and immunity from all interference from without. We hold the land too sacred for any but a Muslim foot. You cannot expect King Hussain to do all that we are entitled to expect from the Caliph and Guardian of the Holy Shrine unless his coffers be filled with money drawn from dominions other than Arabia. The British Government has had to pay £120,000 to King Hussain and £60,000 to Ibn-i-Massud, and still the country is seething with trouble. Can the British Government afford to continue the subsidy? Even if it can, it would be a thankless task, for the Muslim hates to see such relations existing between the guardian of the Shrine and a Power that is not Muslim. The Muslims in India have their own doubts and apprehensions; and they have good reasons to fear that such relations may one day develop into a "vested interest," and what "vested interests" mean in diplomatic language, and how they can be manipulated into meaning anything you please, is no secret. Hedjaz is, as it were, a Muslim house; and if a person refuses to allow the functioning of the government under which he lives to enter into his house, or interfere with his household affairs, so long as he lives in conformity with and obedience to the laws of his land, he is within his legitimate rights.

One of the duties required of the Muslim Caliphate is that of keeping the land of Hedjaz, as far as may be, free from non-Muslim visitors. "The religion of Islam," says the learned divine from whom I have already quoted, "is most charitable in its dealings with the followers of other religions, so much so that it preaches the Divine origin of all religion, but the All-Knowing God was aware that the sacred centre of Islam, the emblem of the Pure Unity of the Divine Being, could not be safe as long as non-Muslims in general were allowed to set even their feet there, because, if they were allowed to enter freely, the enemy among them would be able to work out their evil designs against it. An Arab living thirteen hundred years back could not guess what we see to-day, how those who hanker after worldly power make the mere setting of foot on a soil the pretence for its possession. But God, Who knows the unseen, told the Muslims not to allow the non-Muslims to set their foot in Hedjaz." Is it not a simple truth, free from even the shadow of exaggeration? "Expel the non-Muslim from Jazairat-ul-

Arab" was the dying behest of the Holy Prophet, and after thirteen hundred years the Muslims in India and elsewhere have cogent reasons for believing that the sacred behest of the Prophet has now become violated. And if indeed it be so, is it difficult now to understand the unmistakable hostility shown everywhere towards King Hussain, though he may not be responsible for it? And if this British Government has also been instrumental in a breach of the trust confided to the guardian of Mecca and Medina, is it difficult to understand the unrest in Muslim India? The point in issue is quite clear to me in this case. To secure the safety of the land of Hedjaz and of the institution of pilgrimage a strong garrison is absolutely necessary, together with a strong police force, and the maintenance of a number of departmental organizations for the purpose of ensuring peace, safety, health and comfort. It means the expenditure of a vast revenue. The land of Hedjaz in itself cannot yield it, and the Muslims are averse to the imposition of any kind of assessment or tax on anyone in the Hedjaz. Who is going to provide for all these expenses? Anything in the nature of a subsidy from a non-Muslim Government is not only a most undesirable thing from a political point of view, but also against the teachings of our religion. We cannot say our prayers in a mosque which is maintained by non-Muslim money, and all Muslim mosques in the world are one in symbolism—standing in place of the Holy Shrine of Mecca. How can we say our prayers according to our religion in the proper way if the Holy Place, towards which we turn our prayers, is to be maintained by money from the British Government? This is the meaning of the learned author of the *Spirit of Islam*, Syed Ameer Ali, P.C., in his letter to *The Times* a short time since, when he said that "the Muslims cannot say their prayers rightly if the present condition of Hedjaz continues." The maintenance of the Holy Shrine in Mecca does not mean the maintenance of the Kaaba itself alone, but the maintenance of the Hedjaz, with all the requisites and services that I have outlined above. The Muslim Indians, with their innate respect for authority, wish to place the above facts before the Government as well as the people of this country. They render homage to British rule, they pay taxes and rates, their loyalty has remained unimpeachable till now; and they can guarantee their loyalty in the future as well, because rebellion against the Government is a thing especially prohibited in the Qur-án. On the other hand, they intend to exercise their legitimate rights as subjects, they desire to see the situation in Hedjaz definitely settled at last in accordance with their religion, and they feel that in making this demand they are asking nothing more than their legitimate due. They desire to see the land of Hedjaz, not only under the suzerainty of the Turk, but they also desire to see the seat of the Caliphate strong and powerful enough to meet all the demands of this sacred institution. The terms of the Paris Conference are inadequate for this purpose. Muslims apart, no sensible person would deem them to be so if he had to keep in view the needs of the Caliphate. And if the Central Caliphate Committee in India is opposed to the above terms, as the following cablegram to the Premier would seem to show, their opposition is not unreasonable.

The Central Caliphate Committee, Bombay, emphatically protests against Allied proposals in the Near East Conference, and looks upon them as being in direct variance with Muslim religious obligations and British Premier's pledges[1] to Indian Muslims and with Allies' promises made during war, thus:

---

[1] "Nor are we fighting . . . to deprive Turkey of its capital, or of the rich and renowned lands of Asia Minor and Thrace, which are predominantly Turkish in race."—Mr. Lloyd George, January 5, 1918.

"That the above declaration was specific. It was un-

1. Demilitarization of Straits Zone threatens Turkish national security, leaving her exposed to future enemies.

---

qualified and it was very deliberate. It was made with the consent of all parties in the community. It was not opposed by the Labour Party."—Mr. LLOYD GEORGE, House of Commons, February 26, 1920.

". . . We do not challenge the maintenance of the Turkish Empire in the homelands of the Turkish race with its capital at Constantinople."—Mr. LLOYD GEORGE, January 5, 1918.

THRACE.

Seeing that the Greeks constitute to-day the largest non-Muslim element of all others, it is not an exaggeration to say that the Greeks have always been well treated, and thanks to the generosity and the liberal principles of toleration shown by the Ottoman Empire, they have been able to prosper and to preserve their nationality to the present day. What need to say that, at a time when Turkey dominated immense territories extending as far as the gates of Vienna, she could, had she so wished, have assimilated the Greek element as well as the other non-Mussulman elements that to-day cause her so much injury? Moreover, in those times this system of extermination and assimilation was practised in all Europe. The Greeks of Asia have mingled with the Turks and do not form a separate race. They live in small minorities amid Turkish majorities. The vestiges of a distant past can confer no rights upon the Greeks.

The actual Greek State already oppresses two millions of people, more than half of whom are of Turkish race. In Thrace and Macedonia two millions of Turks groan under a foreign yoke and claim their franchise. All the same, in his blind fury Venizelos does not hesitate to claim vast territories inhabited by Turks, and seems to have had promises made to him to the extent of his

2. Gallipoli and Thrace, including Adrianople, are predominantly Muslim in population and ownership of soil. Greece has no claim to this territory. Assignment of Gallipoli to Greeks is regarded by Muslims as direct menace to the safety of the Turkish capital and seat of Caliphate, and the seed of future wars. It is absolutely inadmissible and incompatible with benevolent designs towards Turkey. The city of Adrianople assigned to Greeks is one held in great esteem by Turks. It possesses many Muslim shrines, held in great veneration by the

---

demands. The fulfilment of these promises would be the height of injustice. In Asia Minor, little Greece will be the cause of continual disturbances, and will never manage to subjugate two million Turks who will not consent to sacrifice themselves for the sake of two hundred thousand Greeks. For, since the Balkan War, 300,000 Greeks have quitted the coasts of Anatolia to go and settle in Greece or else on the islands, while 1,500,000 Turks, fleeing from the atrocities of the Balkan States, have come to settle in Asia Minor. Even before this Greek exodus there were barely 200,000 Greeks in the Vilayet of Smyrna. Moreover, the figures contained in the French Yellow Book, in the work by Vital Cuinet on the subject of Asiatic Turkey, published in 1898, in the *Grande Encyclopédie* and the *Nouveau Larousse*, suffice for the purpose of refuting the figures imagined by Venizelos.

Constantinople itself is a fundamentally Turkish town, and nobody can deny its character as such. Even Lord Robert Cecil acknowledged it recently. The Turks here form three-quarters of the population. In 1356 the Ottoman Turks first set foot on the European continent, and in 1361 they possessed themselves of Adrianople and of Thrace. The Mussulman population of Thrace has such a numerical superiority over the non-Mussulman elements that, all together, they only form a third of the entire population.

Muslims of the world. Ethnically Greece has no claim to its possession; historically and ethnically the city is Turkish, and is, besides, a frontier city of European Turkey, the possession of which by Greeks will allow them to threaten the security of Constantinople and the Turkish Empire. Similarly in the case of Smyrna, semi-internationalizing of its port and city threatens the safety of the whole of Turkish Asia Minor. Muslims cannot allow the probability of the tragedy of the bombardment of Alexandria being repeated in Smyrna. Internationalization of Smyrna and the assignment of Adrianople to Greece can only be regarded as needlessly affording opportunities for further successful aggression against Turkey by her enemies. Smyrna is a Muslim city. There are many Islamic associations and shrines here, while the special *régime* provided for the port by the Near East Conference proposals fetters

---

POPULATION OF THRACE

Territory.	Turks.	Greeks.
Adrianople (once capital of the Ottoman Empire) ..	122,725	37,521
Kirk-Killisse	100,979	31,611
Rodosto	107,533	25,013
Dimotika	84,568	39,867
Dedegatch	39,660	24,620
Goumuldjine	238,277	21,735
Nevrekop	114,928	19,434
Seres	183,000	78,000
Drama	163,132	25,411
Totals	1,154,802	303,212

The Muslim Standard, April 26, 1922.

Turkish independence in the matter of control of customs and trade passing through the greatest mart in Asia Minor and one of the chief ports of the Ottoman Empire. Internationalization of Smyrna would gratuitously sow the seed of future invasions of Asia Minor, and would menace safety of Turkey in Asia and the Ottoman Empire.

3. The suggested ratification of capitulations imposed by the Sèvres Treaty cripples and enslaves Turkey financially, and conflicts with the conception of Turkey as an independent State.

4. Specific restoration of legal rights of Caliphate of Muslims over Holy Places pledged by England to the Muslim world is ignored. Religious obligations compel Muslims to insist on this point.

5. Freedom of Jazirat-ul-Arab—namely, Syria, Mesopotamia, Palestine, and Arabia — from non-Muslim domination and control is likewise not provided for in accordance with England's pledges. To the Islamic world this is religious obligation on which there can be no compromise.

6. Proposals referred to in 1, 2, 3, 4, and 5, above, are in direct variance with the British Premier's historic pledge of January, 1918, given to the Muslims of India and the world regarding complete independence of Turkish homelands. Thus de-militarization of the Straits Zone constitutes a standing menace to the Turkish capital and nation. Establishment of Greek rule in that portion of Thrace including Adrianople and in Gallipoli means placing a portion of the Turkish homelands under Greek rule. Internationalization of Smyrna endangers the safety of the whole of Asia Minor. Ratification of capitulations imposed by the Sèvres Treaty will bind Turkey to financial and economic slavery to European Powers benefiting by these capitulations.

How far the French Premier believed in the

acceptability of the terms appears from his following comment:

> They are merely offers of mediation and wise counsel from the Allies, and in no sense an ultimatum. The Foreign Ministers were inspired by a desire not to offend either of the adversaries. "If Turkey, considering that the frontier proposed in Thrace does not come up to her aspirations, rejects the proposals, we would not come to a deadlock," added M. Poincaré, "and it would always be possible to restart the conversations on another basis."—*Yorkshire Post*, March 27, 1922.

An English friend writes to me the following in a personal letter:

THE PARIS PROPOSALS.

Those with regard to Thrace and the Straits are, in my humble opinion, very bad.

The proposals with regard to the Straits are not at all clear to me. I confess I do not understand them. I cannot either from *The Times* summary or from Marquis Curzon's speech in the House of Lords understand what is the position in the Gallipoli peninsula.

The Asiatic shore of the Dardanelles is to be left to the Turks, but demilitarized to a depth of 60 miles.

The Gallipoli peninsula is to be given to the Greeks, to be administered by them as a part of Greece, but it is to be demilitarized and an international force stationed there to assure free access and passage through the Straits.

All the forts are apparently to be destroyed, and the object of the international force is to assure free access and passage by seeing that these forts are not rebuilt.

If the international force is to be there without forts, then of course Constantinople is left at the mercy of any hostile fleet. There would be nothing to prevent a

Greek fleet passing any night through the Straits and blowing Constantinople to pieces in the morning. The Powers might object, but in view of the *fait accompli* would do nothing.

I cannot believe that the international force is intended to be powerless to prevent a *coup d'état* of this sort. I think this point requires clearing up.

If it is so, of course the possession of Constantinople to the Turks is worthless and a continued temptation to attack. Once Constantinople was either taken or destroyed, the Turkish army in Thrace would be cut off and at the mercy of the Greeks or of any other Power who had steamed through the Straits.

If the Straits are to be demilitarized in such a way that any fleet of warships can pass through without difficulty or molestation, it is farcical to suppose that Constantinople can remain the seat of the Caliphate or the capital city of the Ottoman Empire.

The proposals to divide Eastern Thrace are extremely unjust, and I cannot see how the Turks can accept them. They do not fulfil Mr. Lloyd George's very solemn pledges to the Moslems of India, which the Turks relied upon when they unconditionally surrendered. Turkish statistics show that 84 per cent. of the land in Eastern Thrace is owned by Turks, and of the population 67·5 is Turkish, 25·5 Greek, and 5·0 Bulgar and Armenian.

The Greek census of 1921 showed the total population of Eastern Thrace to be nearly 500,000. Of these the Constantinople *Times* correspondent, who cannot be accused of partiality towards Turkey, estimated 300,000 were Turks, that is, only 7 per cent. less than shown by the Turkish figures. As regards Western Thrace, the population there is, so I understand, even more preponderatingly Turkish than Eastern Thrace.

The proposal to surrender Adrianople to Greece is a scandal. *The Times* correspondent already referred to has admitted that it is essentially a Turkish town, and that 70 per cent. of the population is Turkish; it is a town especially endeared to Muslims on account of its great historical and religious associations; nor are Muslims ever likely to forget or forgive the behaviour of the Greek inhabitants when the Turks, in the Balkan War, after a most gallant resistance, were starved into surrender. As recounted in the *Carnegie Report*, ch. iii. 109–116, these dirty hounds swarmed out of their cellars and hiding places, looted the undefended property of the Turks, pillaged and desecrated the glorious Sultan Selim Mosque, and wilfully destroyed and tore in pieces the priceless manuscripts in the great Oriental Library. Indeed, the Marquis Curzon has strange ideas of what is seemly and right and just. The projection of Greek territory between Turkey and Bulgaria is a deliberate provocation to Turk and Bulgar to combine. Even should the Turks accept under duress the Paris proposals with regard to Thrace, it will only mean that the seed of another war is ready to sprout.

CHAPTER IX

MUSLIM INTERESTS IN PALESTINE

NEXT in sanctity to Mecca, in the eye of the Muslim, comes Jerusalem. According to us, there are two places in the world which have been dedicated to the worship of God from remotest antiquity. One is the "Masjid-ul-Haram" at Mecca, the other the "Masjid-ul-Aqsa" at Jerusalem. A Muslim when making his pilgrimage to Mecca is expected also to make pilgrimage to Jerusalem. The phrase, "Haji-ul-Huramain Sharifain" signifies that the bearer of the epithet has made his pilgrimage to the two sacred houses, that is to say, Mecca and Jerusalem. In Muslim parlance, "Bait-ul-Muqaddas" (The Sacred House) or "Quds" (The Sacred) is the name commonly given to Jerusalem. So much so, indeed, that while Jerusalem is a strange word to more than three-fourths of the Muslims in the world, the other two names are household words in all Muslim lands. Besides the "Hararm-Sherif," there is another very famous Muslim sanctuary at "Khalil-ur-Rahman"—Hebron, where Abraham and the three other prophets of his family lie buried. Muslim shrines, indeed, are dotted all about the country, and among them are to be found the burial-places of some of the Prophet's companions. I visited nearly all these places, and found Jerusalem a veritable Holy Land for Islam. I saw places and scenes in the town and its surroundings which helped me to understand many verses in the Qur-án far more clearly than I could have done before. "The Prophet Muhammad was carried by night in a vision from the House of God at Mecca to the House of God at Jerusalem, and thence up through the Seven Heavens to the very Source of Light; and pious Muslims, remembering that grand vision of celestial majesty, think of Jerusalem as the foot of a mystic stairway, leading up to the Divine abode. The early Muslims, in the first days, turned their faces towards Jerusalem in their prayer." [1]

Three great nations have their religious interests in Palestine—Jews, Christians, and Muslims. Is it not our first duty, then, to find out which of these three is best suited to guard the interests of the others? History and the respective beliefs of the parties concerned

[1] Marmaduke Pickthall.

can decide this question. Jews do not believe in Jesus, and can by religion have no veneration for places sacred to Christianity. A Christian has no faith in Islam, and cannot be expected to pay the same respect to Muslim Holy Places as a Muslim would do. The case of a Muslim is quite different. Every holy name of importance in Jerusalem is holy to him. Every prophet that was raised up in Jerusalem and in its vicinity is his own prophet. There are various verses in the Qur-án which support my statement, but I will give here only a part of section 10 of chap. vi.:

> (84) And this was our argument, which we gave to Abraham against his people. . . . (85) And we gave to him Isaac, and Jacob, each did we guide, and Noah did we guide before, and of his descendants David, and Solomon, and Job, and Joseph, and Moses, and Aaron; . . . (86) and Zacharias, and John, and Jesus, and Elias; every one was of the good; (87) and Ishmail, and Elishah, and Jonas, and Lot; . . . (88) and from among their fathers, and their descendants, and their brethren, and we chose them and guided them into the right path . . . (91) These are they whom God guided, therefore follow their guidance.

Eighteen prophets are named here, and do they not include every sacred name which has some connection with Palestine? A Muslim is told in the last verse to follow the guidance of all the prophets and respect them as his own, and he has to make no distinction between prophet and prophet under the injunction of the Qur-án (ii. 120).

Think over the names I have stated in the quoted verses. Can you suggest to me any other name whose holy memories have some connection with Palestine and which the Qur-ánic list does not include? A Muslim has to respect them all, and to regard them as his own prophets. Can a Jew entertain the same ideas of veneration for these places which belong to Christians and Muslims, and can a Christian share with the Muslim the respect which the latter cherishes for places hallowed by his traditions and religion? Read the whole of your sacred Scriptures, and point out to me a single verse or a sentence in the whole writing which inculcates such broad-minded respect for the prophets and spiritual teachers of other religions.

All this shows clearly enough that Palestine is our Holy Land too; and those who cannot understand why the Muslims in India include Jerusalem among their claims may find something in what I have written here to induce them to revise their judgment.

In addition to the contentions of Indian Muslims concerning Jerusalem, the Arab delegation from Palestine—in London now—is reminding the nation of the pledges given to them—the inhabitants of Palestine—by the British Government. Leaving aside the solemn pledges of Mr. Asquith, whereby, as the Prime Minister of England, he undertook that no non-Muslim Power should ever be permitted to intermeddle with Palestine, the Arabs have, since, been definitely promised independent and self-determined States in Palestine, Hedjaz, Syria and Irak-e-Arab. Every effort towards Zionism is nothing more nor less than a violation of those pledges. Policies of this kind may be proper enough for the West, where treaties have ever been more honoured in the breach than in the observance; but here is a matter in which you have to deal with the East, and, more especially, with Muslims, in whose eyes the pledged word stands above every other thing. It is a most regrettable circumstance that, wherever we find unrest in these days under British rule, its source may be traced to a broken pledge —a pledge given in time of trouble, for the purpose of securing help; and the help came, on the strength of that pledge; and then, when the trouble is over, and you enjoy the fruits of that help, the pledge is forgotten. In India, in Palestine, in every country where discontent prevails, the people are simply reminding the Government of broken promises. The East believes in the supremacy of moral order over all else. I have been in Palestine, Syria and Hedjaz. I have visited the Straits Settlements, Java and Burma. I have met with people of every nationality. Wherever I went I found Muslims respecting English people, because they were truthful and in the habit of keeping their word, more than they respected any other Western nation. It is a keen sense of disappointment which has, more than anything else, aggravated the unrest. From a Muslim point of view the rulers and the ruled are parties to a contract, under which it is the former's duty to look to the safety of the life, property and general interest of the latter, and the latter's to pay the taxes lawfully demanded and submit to authority. The contract cannot be respected if one of the parties thereto is found incapable of respecting its word.[1]

There is yet another aspect of the question.

[1] The recently published observations of the Central Khilafat (Caliphate) Committee, Bombay, and the Indian Government Press communiqué issued in connection with the Paris Conference proposals substantiate these remarks. The said Committee not only doubts the genuineness, but shows also the hollowness, of the Government assurance to respect Muslim demands in the face of Lord Curzon's proposals. They again remind of the said pledges, and find their breach in the said Conference. As to the question of Palestine, they cannot bear to see Arabs under Jewish rule, which, they think, will be he ultimate result of the Zionist scheme.

If you have to deal with a Muslim nation, you must scrupulously respect their religious susceptibilities. A Muslim can tolerate no interference with his religion. It is religion which is at the root of the Caliphate agitation. I need not dwell further upon the fulfilment of your pledges to the Arabs in Palestine. Many honourable lords and gentlemen of both Houses have become alive to the injustice which would be involved by the execution of the Balfour declaration. I state here the question in its general aspect, from the Muslim point of view, which should be rightly appreciated to bring the present unrest to end. If the maintenance and continuance of the Caliphate, in the sense I have already explained, as well as the immunity of Hedjaz from non-Muslim interference is a Divine promise to Muslims, given in the Qur-án, we read also a similar promise in the book concerning Palestine.

> And most certainly We wrote in the Book after the reminder that (as for) the land, My righteous servants shall inherit it (Qur-án, xxi. 105).

The land referred to in the verse is the Holy Land, and the promise as to the possession of it by the Muslims was fulfilled in the Caliphate of Omar. In Zionism the Muslims see an effort to violate the above-quoted words of God; and they think themselves bound therefore to strive their utmost to put an end to the scheme.

Zionism, without the restoration of the Temple of Solomon to its original condition is an absurdity; and so to restore the Temple is a task impossible without the destruction of the Great Mosque of Omar. The Mosque has been built on the roof of the Temple, and the worshippers going into the Mosque have to walk on the roof of the Temple. They also must traverse a piece of land under which lies the Sanctuary of Sanctuaries, in the eye of the Jew, which ought not to be trodden by human foot. I found the Jews standing on a certain wall and not going beyond it, and on my inquiry I was told that to go beyond it is sacrilege, for there lies the Sanctuary buried beneath the ground. The same I saw when I visited the tomb of the prophet Abraham at Khalil-ur-Rahman, I found half a dozen Jew pilgrims standing half-way on the flight of stairs leading to the sanctuary of the father of the nations, and for the same reason. The sacrilege is continually being committed by the Muslims and the Christians of the day on their way towards "Sakhrá" (the Sacred Rock) or to the Mosque of Omar; and I am afraid I was also guilty of the same. Could you see Zionism established in Jerusalem if the Sanctuary and the Temple are not to be restored to their former position, thereby giving the greatest conceivable offence to Muslim susceptibilities? But if Zionism means simply the finding of a national home for the Jews, they have found already in the Muslim empire a home and refuge from the persecution of the Western Christians. Others might have followed them had they been permitted to become Ottoman subjects.

CHAPTER X

THE CALIPHATE AND ITS CLAIMANTS

THE enthronement of Syed Hussain as King of the Hedjaz should not be confused with the question of the Caliphate. Syed Hussain as the King of Hedjaz and Syed Hussain as the custodian of the Holy Shrines on behalf of the Khalifa-tul-Muslameen, are two distinct and separate entities. He has also renounced his claim to the Caliphate in favour of the Turks, as we read in *Kaaba*, the local journal at Mecca.

It is instructive to note how Turcophobia—aggravated by ignorance—tends to make men normally sensible appear as though devoid of common sense, to say nothing of judgment. On the one hand we have a statement to the effect that the Turkish Caliphate will not be agreeable to the Shiaites, because the Turks belong to the Sunni sect of Islam; and on the other, a contention equally authoritative, that King Hussain is the obvious and most suitable person for the office of Caliph. These latter, perhaps, forget, if they ever knew, the circumstance that King Hussain, like the Turks, is a Sunni. They must also have forgotten, if they ever knew, that sectarianism, as that term is understood in England, is non-existent in Islam, and must not be confused with the idea of Christian sects. In the sense in which the word "sect" is used in Christendom there is no sect in Islam. The word "sect" cannot properly be applied to the various so-called "schools of thought" in Islam. All Muslims, be they *Sunnis* or *Shias*, *Wahabis* or *Muqullid*, believe in the Oneness of God and the Messengership of the Holy Prophet. They accept the Qur-án and the sayings and acts of the Prophet as the sole source of authority and guidance. All the Islamic laws, ethics and ritual have their source in God and the Prophet, and whatever has reached us from these two sources is one and the same everywhere in the Muslim world. All Muslims believe in the five pillars of Islam and the seven principles of Faith; they keep their face towards Kaaba when they pray; all their prayers and ceremonies of praying, recitations, their gesticulations and prostrations in prayer, are after the ordinance and example of the Prophet, and in these all Muslims agree. In short, that which constitutes Islam and the Faith is the same throughout the whole Muslim world. The points of difference, if such they can be called, in the sects of Islam are of very minor importance as far as Faith goes. Take, for example, the case of the Shias and the Sunnis. Their main difference begins after the death of the Prophet, and is more of politics than of Faith. The Shias maintain that rightful successorship to the Prophet could only be claimed by Hazrat Ali and his descendants, and not by Hazrat Abu Bakr, Omar and Osman; but at the same time they believe that Hazrat Ali did not do any wrong in accepting Hazrat Abu Bakr, Omar and Osman successively as Caliphs of the Faith. Hazrat Ali was the fourth Caliph, and yet he paid his allegiance and homage to the first three. The thing may seem to be paradoxical to a Western politician, who is ever seeking pretexts for disqualifying the Turks for the Caliphate; but to us Muslims the situation is quite clear, seeing that the Caliphate goes by election and not by descent. We Muslims of to-day hold the same principle. For the last thirteen hundred years the Caliphate and the guardianship of the Holy Places has been in the hands of the Sunyites, including the Kerbela and Kazamain—the two places of special sacredness to the Shiaites—and yet the

Muslim conscience is never perturbed by any suggestions, except such as come from the Christian camp.

I may usefully, in this connection, refer to the attitude of the three notable Shias in London, who have spared no pains in supporting the cause of the Turkish Caliphate. I mean H.H. the Agha Khan, the Right Hon. Syed Amir Ali, P.C., and Nazim-ut-tajjar Mirza Hashim Ispahani. The institution of the Caliphate is chiefly concerned with the safety and upkeep of the Holy Shrines in the manner I have explained, and sectarianism, if any, of Islam plays no part in it.

Similarly, the question of descent from the Holy Prophet is of minor importance in the selection of the Caliph.

Those who are imbued with democratic principles in religion, as well as in other things, set no exaggerated value on lineage, for ancestry is of no consequence in Islam. As the Qur-án says:

> O, you men, surely We have created you of a male and a female and made you tribes and families that you may know each other; surely the most honourable of you with Allah is the one among you most careful (of his duty). Surely Allah is Knowing, Aware (xlix. 13).

The Holy Prophet says the same thing. To his own beloved daughter Fatima, through whom his descendants were to spread all over the world, he was reported to have said, "You will be asked to account for your actions, and not for who was your father." Could there be clearer authority than these quotations for contradicting the foolish notion current in the English Press, that the Muslims would hail a Caliphate with a descendant of the Prophet at its head? The question of the Caliphate is a purely Muslim question, not by any means obscure, and well-meaning friends here need not offer the light of their candles where there is no darkness at all. Such suggestions are apt to arouse not only resentment, but also suspicion as to the *bona fides* of the persons making them. Apart altogether from any learned discussion or academic theory on the question, the mere fact that Muslims of all countries have willingly consented to the Turkish Caliphate for the last five hundred years is sufficient to show the futility of the Qureshite theory. Not only have Muslims under non-Muslim rule paid homage to the Sultan as the Muslim Caliph, but Muslim emperors in India, as well as in other lands, have, without murmur, bowed to the Caliphate of Turkey. The Seljuk kings and the Moghul emperors, even in their palmy days, admitted the right of the Sultan to the Caliphate, so much so that their disputes among themselves were referred to him for arbitration.

The Qureshite theory is, however, not entirely without some show of authority; and it seems a pity that responsible persons, here as well as in India, should have been hunting for such authority long before the conclusion of the war.

The same verse in the Qur-án which speaks of the Caliphate, speaks also of its functions and the qualifications of the Caliph:

> Allah has promised to those of you who believe and do good that He will most certainly make them Caliphas.

"Who believe and do good." Here is summed up the main qualification of a Caliph, and this can be claimed and possessed by every Muslim, whether he trace his descent to the Prophet or to an Abyssinian or a Tartar. One of the chief duties of the Caliph is the guardianship of the Holy Places; as the Qur-án says:

> And what excuse have they that Allah should not chastise them while they hinder men from the Sacred Mosque, and they are not fit to be guardians of it; its guardians are only the Muttaqi people (viii. 34).

The word *Muttaqi* means "righteous." Here righteousness is made the sole qualification for the guardianship of the Holy Places, and not the descent of the guardian from the

Prophet. The first four Caliphs, those immediately after the Prophet, were not the descendants of the Prophet, nor were the Ommayyides and Abbasides. With the exception of Hassan, the Prophet's grandson, and the one or two Caliphs of the Fatimites, for a small interval of time between the Abbasides and the Turks, when the Fatimites claimed it, the Caliphate has always been in the hands of those who did not descend from the Prophet. We do, in fact, in certain of the sayings of the Prophet, find some mention of the Qureshite Caliphate; but that does not affect the position of the non-Qureshite Caliphate. Even as early as the days of Omar, the Hadis of the Qureshite Caliphate was not taken to be exclusive in its significance. Omar, the second Caliph, is reported to have said that if, at his death, Abu Obeida should be alive, he would make him Caliph, but if Abu Obeida was dead, and Moáz, son of Jabal, alive, he would make Moáz Caliph. Moáz did not come from the Qureshite stock, and if Omar had known that the Caliphate ought to be the privilege of the Qureshite exclusively, he could hardly propose to name Moáz as a fit candidate for the Caliphate. If the Prophet spoke of the Qureshite Caliphs he also prophesied their number. He said that the ascendancy of Islam would remain during the reigns of the twelve Caliphs, and that all the twelve would be from the Qureshites. The prophecy was fulfilled, and the last of the Ommayyides was the twelfth Qureshite Caliph. On the other hand, it does not show that there will be no other Qureshites after the Ommayyides. The Prophet prophesied about the Caliphate of his tribe in connection with the ascendancy of Islam. The Qureshites were the noble tribe in Arabia and the fittest persons for the post in those days, commanding, as they did, the respect and allegiance of the rest, at a time when the principle of election was quite a new thing to the aristocratic Arabs. In short, the Muslim Caliphate is not a family affair. It is open to everyone who may perform its duties, but subject to the universal consent of the Muslim world. The consensus in the present case is in favour of Turkey. King Hussain himself lays no claim to the Caliphate. He bows to the universal consensus of opinion, as I said before. The Palestine Muslims, the Mujtihads of Persia and the Ulemas of Baghdad and Kerbela all are unanimous in favour of the Sultan.

Those who advocate King Hussain are not only guilty of officiousness, but may be suspected of sinister motives to the detriment of Islam. The following I quote from the letter of Mr. Arthur Moore, the well-known traveller in the East, from Kabul, published in *The Times* of April 24, 1922, which may be read with great advantage, and which may help many to appreciate the importance of the question:

> Leading Afghans in conversation all insist on the strength of the feeling throughout the country with regard to the Caliphate; they reject Arab suzerainty over the Holy Places and express dislike of the Sherif of Mecca. One Sirdar quoted to me a Persian proverb, "If you shut a man up in a room, you force him finally to break down the door," as typifying the desperate position, at the present time, of Islam, which is drawn together everywhere by misfortune, and, convinced that the world is drifting towards another great war, awaits an opportunity for venting its despair.

The Indebtedness of the British Government to the Turkish Caliphate

We need not go back to the days of Queen Elizabeth, when her Government sought the alliance and help of Turkey against Spaniards. The Caliphate in those days was at its prime, and its friendship was courted by every Western Power. The end of the eighteenth century saw the tug-of-war between the French and the British for the supremacy in India. The British sought the alliance of Sultan Tippu against the French, and the British authorities of those times fortunately had a more intimate knowledge of the Caliphate and its influence on the Muslim rulers of the world than would seem to have been vouchsafed to the present Government. Mr. Spencer was then the Ambassador at Constantinople, and it was he who requested the Porte to exercise its influence with Sultan Tippu. Sultan Selim III wrote a long letter on September 20, 1798, in Arabic, which reached Tippu on January 15, 1799, with another letter from the Marquis Wellesley, the then Governor-General of the East India Company. In these letters, as well as in the reply from Tippu to Sultan Selim, the Turkish Sultan was referred to and addressed as Caliph of Islam; and his religious suzerainty over the Muslims of the whole world was without question admitted. Again, in the days of the Mutiny in India, the Earl of Beaconsfield found it advisable to approach the Sultan, who willingly came to help the British cause in India. There are thousands of Muslims still alive in India who heard the Firman (Royal Dispatch) of the Sultan read to them in the mosques just after the Mutiny, exhorting them to pay their allegiance to the British rule, and now are lost in wonder at the present attitude of the British Cabinet towards the Sultan, its old and tried ally.

The Turks and the Caliphate

If the Muslims of the world are so greatly attached to Turkey they have good reasons to be so. The Caliphate changed hands at a time when the Muslims had been everywhere hard pressed. The Abbáside power had become extinct, and the Fátimite rule in Egypt was in weak hands; the Moors had been driven from Spain, and the Muslim lands in Northern Africa became victims to Spanish and Portuguese onslaughts, subject to constant invasion and despoilment. Even the Muslim territories on the seacoast of India were not free from Portuguese piracy. Just at that juncture Sultan Sulaimán appeared on the scene. He was followed by his famous son Selim, who ruled for only three years, and died in 923 A.H., being succeeded by his son Sulaimán the Great. In his days almost every Muslim Power was in alliance with Turkey. They asked the Sultan for help when in need, and referred all disputes among themselves to his arbitration. Sultan Selim and his son Sulaimán came to the rescue of the Muslims, and very soon the Muslim territories on the coasts of Africa and India were freed from Spanish and Portuguese depredation. The Friday sermon was read in the name of the Turkish Sultan as Caliph of

Islam in every mosque in the Muslim world. The Muslim power was everywhere at its height at that time. Those were the days when the Mogul Empire reached the zenith of its splendour in India. But the great Muslim emperors and kings, all the world over, when attending the Friday prayer had to listen willingly to the Friday sermon in the terms I have mentioned. The sermon, in its concluding portion, made mention first of the Prophet, then of the first four Caliphs, and then of the existing ruler of Turkey as the Caliph of Islam. And to-day I have seen the same in my travels in Burma, Malay and Java, besides India. One thing is especially noteworthy in this respect, and that is, that in works of history, biography, travel and the like, as well as in Royal Firmans, the names of various kings are mentioned as occasion demanded in connection with and as rulers of their respective countries; but where mention is made of the Turkish Sultan he is invariably styled Caliph of Islam and the Defender of the Religion for the whole world. Even the great Muslim divines, in their references to the Sultan, use the same phraseology. We read thus in *Zafaralwalah*, an Arabic history of Gujarati, by Muhammad Assifi: "At this time the ruler of Turkey was the Sultan of Islam; he is the Caliph (Viceroy) of

God in the whole world, and he is Sulaimán Khan, son of Selim Khan . . ." (page 316). Again, King Humayou, in his discourse with the Turkish Admiral Syed Ali, is said to have observed: "Indeed the ruler of Turkey deserves to be called the King of the World, and no other ruler can claim that title." King Shershah, of Súr dynasty, and Emperor Shah Jehan speak in similar terms when they refer to the Sultan in their dispatches and other writings. I think I have said enough to show why Muslims of the world favour Turkey in this matter of the Caliphate. But her real claim to that office lies elsewhere, that is, in her services to the Holy Shrines and to the pilgrims. The Sultan neither styles himself the Monarch of Hedjaz nor the Religious Magnate of the Muslims. He is proud to call himself *Khadim-ul-Harmen Sharifen*—the Servant of the Holy Places; and, indeed, so he has proved to be. Arabia has never been a source of revenue to Turkey, and if at times some of the chiefs of Arabia have been disposed to revolt against Turkish suzerainty, and the Turk has not taken much notice of it, it was for the reason that he never counted on any revenue from Arabia; their chief concern was to maintain peace in the land of Hedjaz, and to keep it free from disturbance, so as to enable the pilgrims from the Muslim world to perform their pilgrimage and live in the Holy Places in peace and comfort. But when the tribal insurrection threatened the peace of the Holy Land, then Turkey had to subdue it, as in duty bound.

No pains, in short, were ever spared to secure peace, safety and comfort to the pilgrims during these five hundred years, and the Turks therefore do deserve the support of the whole Muslim world in the matter of Caliphate.

Though the conduct of King Hussain has aroused public censure throughout the Muslim world, yet, in the opinion of many, the course he has adopted was under the pressure of circumstances inevitable.

The Hedjaz is, as I have said, a barren land, with no cultivation, and its inhabitants depend for their sustenance solely on the produce of other countries.

The importation of food-stuffs from Syria —their main, or rather, perhaps, their only source of supply—was cut off during the war, and the people there were thrown on the compassion of the Allies for the very means of bare existence.

Arabia was, more or less, under blockade, and the ex-Shereef had no choice but to accede to the demands of the Allies.. If there had been no other reason for this course, the very lives of his people would have compelled him to it. But that is now ancient history. As regards the future, many hold that his position as King of the Hedjaz will not be much affected, one way or another, if the Caliphate, with its necessary accompanying suzerainty of Arabia, reverts to Turkey. Her pre-war possession of the country brought her no great revenue, for the inhabitants of Mecca and Medina were never subject to taxation, nor were the pilgrims; but Turkey, on the other hand, had to spend her own revenue in the service of the Holy Shrines.

The existence of a number of principalities in Arabia before the war could not affect the Caliphate and the Turkish suzerainty, nor is it likely that the newly created kingdom of Hedjaz could be of much consequence to Turkey, provided, that is to say, that the Hedjaz remains for ever free from foreign interference and foreign diplomacy, and provided also that the King of the Hedjaz has no direct diplomatic relations with other Powers. The same may be said of the new kingdom in Iráq.

The Muslim desire is, so far as I am able to crystallize it, to see *Jazirat-ul-Arab* and the land of Hedjaz free from non-Muslim influences and elements, and they desire to see this a *fait accompli*, in fulfilment of the words of the Prophet which I have quoted elsewhere.

I see no reason why these words should not be respected by the British Government, if Great Britain claims to be the greatest Muslim empire in the world; that being done, the Turks can easily come to terms with King Hussain. It is vital to his interests that he should win the good will of the Muslim world, which I have reasons to believe will be forthcoming; and in aiding him in this way to win that good will, Great Britain will be adding enormously to her power and prestige in the Muslim lands, populated by Muslims, over which she rules.

To foment rivalry between Arab and Turk will not pay in the long run. All efforts to lower the prestige of the Turks in the eyes of the world have simply had the contrary effect. To-day they are far nearer to Muslim hearts throughout the world than they ever were before; and if the Government is genuinely interested in the stability of the Arab States it must take steps to create cordial relations between the Arabs and the Turks. I have reason to believe that such a policy will help immensely towards allaying the tension which is increasing every day among the Indian Muslims. The task of reconciling the Muslim to the kingship of Hussain is by no means a hopeless one, and it can be accomplished with no great difficulty, if the Turks are but permitted to come to some sort of understanding with the King of Hedjaz.

CHAPTER XI

NON-MUSLIMS UNDER MUSLIM RULE

Of late, much has been said in the Press about Christian minorities under the Turkish rule. It is alleged that the Turkish code of law, based on the Qur-ánic jurisprudence thirteen hundred years old, must of necessity be unsuitable for progressive nations of to-day; hence the plea for bringing Armenians and Greeks in Turkey under a special *régime*, acting in accordance with supervisory powers vested in the League of Nations. It is further alleged that the Qur-ánic and Muslim law cannot be fair to non-Muslim subjects. Unfortunately, these contentions emanate from persons who have little time to study the subject before hazarding their opinions. It may be that they regard Islam somewhat in the same light as the Christian bigotry of the Middle Ages, and it is not surprising that a fellow-subject in Islam should fail to find any justification for such a charge. To him that charge and all that it implies must be baseless, because he has good reason to believe that "no conquering race or faith has given to its subjects a nobler guarantee than is to be found in the following words of the Prophet"[1]:

> To the Christians of Najran and the neighbouring territories, the security of God and the pledge of His Prophet are extended for their lives, their religion and their property—to the present as well as the absent and others besides: there shall be no interference with (the practice of) their faith or their observances; nor any change in their rights or privileges; no bishop shall be removed from his bishopric, nor any monk from his monastery, nor any priest from his priesthood, and they shall continue to enjoy everything great and small as heretofore; no image or cross shall be destroyed; they shall not oppress or be oppressed; they shall not practise the rights of blood-vengeance as in the Days of Ignorance; no tithes shall be levied from them, nor shall they be required to furnish provisions for the troops.

After the subjugation of Hira in the days of Abu Bakr, the first Caliph, Khalid-bin-Walid, the Muslim commander, issued a proclamation by which he guaranteed the lives, liberty and property of the Christians, and declared that "they shall not be prevented from beating their *nakus*, and taking out their crosses on occasions of festivals." This declaration was approved of and sanctioned by the Caliph and his council. After the conquest of

[1] Syed Ameer Ali, P.C., *The Spirit of Islam.*

Egypt the Caliph Omar scrupulously preserved intact the property dedicated to the Christian churches, and continued the allowance made by the formal government for the support of the priest. In the reign of Osman, the third Caliph, the Christian Patriarch of Merv bears the following testimony to the tolerant spirit of the Muslims, in his letter to Bishop Simeon of Fars:

> The Arabs, who have been given by God the kingdom (of the earth), do not attack the Christian faith; on the contrary, they help us in our religion; they respect our God and our saints and bestow gifts on our churches and monasteries.

Adverse critics of Islam have something here to think upon. Could they conceive of even a semblance of such tolerance in their own annals? Even at the present time, if the Muslims wished to build a mosque in London and were to approach the Government with a view to assistance, it is more than probable that opposition would be forthcoming from the official custodians of Christian conscience, charity and meekness.

The following extract from the *Rangoon Daily News* is of interest in this connection, and we may be excused for feelings of surprise at the information which is disclosed in the words I have italicized:

In the House of Commons Sir J. W. Rees drew attention to the Muslim mosque which is being built at Paris, and suggested that a mosque should be provided in London as soon as financial conditions allowed.

Mr. Harmsworth replied that there were *several mosques* in England, and even if there were room for another he did not think it a matter for Government expenditure, but he promised to inquire what was happening in France.

In Islam the Muslims and the *Zimmis*[1] are absolutely equal in the eyes of the law.

"Their blood," said Ali, the fourth Caliph, "was like our blood." "Many modern governments," says the learned author of the *Spirit of Islam*, "not excepting some of the most civilized, may take the Muslim administrations for their model." In the punishment of crime there was no difference between the rulers and the ruled. I have already cited the instance of King Jabala, under the rule of Caliph Omar. This is the law of Islam, that if a Zimmi is killed by a Muslim the latter is liable to the same penalty as in the reverse case.

In permitting non-Muslims to hold positions of trust, Islam has shown a unique largeness

[1] The non-Muslim subjects of Muslim States are called Zimmis. The word itself is very instructive, and shows the immunity which a non-Muslim enjoys under the Muslim rule. The word means "people living under guarantees," i.e. every Muslim is responsible for the safety of the life, liberty and property of the non-Muslim.

of mind seldom to be met with elsewhere. Even in the first century of the Muslim era we find important offices of State held by the Christians, the Jews and the Magians. They were even appointed rectors of Muslim universities and educational institutions, and curators of Muslim endowments, provided only that they did not perform any religious functions. The Abbasides, and the dynasties that followed them, recognized no distinction on the score of religion. Under the Mogul emperors of Delhi, Hindus commanded armies, administered finance, governed provinces, and sat in the councils of the sovereign. The Turks of the present day have not been lacking in a like spirit of generosity, and have long allowed Armenians to hold posts [1] which the British government in India would never till now have dreamed of entrusting to an Indian.

After the Qur-án the words of the Prophet are final. "There shall be no interference with their (Christian) faith, or their observance; nor any change in their rights and privileges." So runs the charter given by the Prophet to the Christians of the Najran, and its terms are such as to leave no shadow of a right of a Muslim ruler to interfere with the personal or religious liberty of his non-Muslim subjects. The Turkish Sultan cannot

[1] See Appendix V.

disregard this charter, as successor to the Prophet, and I cannot conceive what these much-talked-of Christian minorities can, in reason, demand from the Turks more than the rights and privileges that come within the purview of the charter. As to the change of religion and its penalty under a Muslim rule, there need be no misgiving. In Islam there is no penalty for apostasy.[1]

The Turkish rule may not be a model, but the legends current concerning it for the last fifty years have proved, in the upshot, to be after all mere stories deliberately concocted of set purpose to provide a pretext for the dismemberment of Turkey. His Excellency M. Chedo Miyatovich, formerly Minister to the Court of St. James and to the Sublime Porte, writing in the *Asiatic Quarterly* (October 1913), after Serbia had at last succeeded in realizing her "aspirations," so far as Turkey was concerned, candidly admitted that:

> *Political interest made us* (the Balkan nations) *paint the Turks as cruel tyrants incapable of European civilization.* An impartial history would prove that the Turks are rather Europeans than Asiatics, and that they are not cruel tyrants, but a nation loving justice and fairness, and possessing qualities and virtues which deserve to be acknowledged and respected.

The italics furnish an eloquent explanation

[1] See Appendix I.

of the motives actuating those writers who have poured forth book after book to justify foreign interference in Turkey, and who do not fail to write in the dailies here. Unrest, dissatisfaction, or movements towards self-government on the part of subject races, cannot be taken as proof positive of the incapacity of the existing government to govern. But if the symptoms be admissible as evidence against the capacity of the Turk to rule the heterogeneous mass of people under him, what shall be said of the capacity of the British people to rule, when unrest has been rampant in India, Ceylon and elsewhere? Are the advocates of a special treatment for the Greeks and the Armenians in Turkey prepared to recommend a similar panacea for India and Ceylon? The thing is inconceivable to any thinking person—and yet I could wish that those persons who experience no difficulty in accounting for the present unfortunate position in India on grounds that reflect no discredit on British rule, but rather the reverse, could see their way, in fairness, to apply a like method, *mutatis mutandis,* to the affairs of Turkey. As regards the prosperity of the people under Turkish rule, much has been said to that rule's discredit; but, leaving aside the question of how far these statements are true, what are the real causes of such a state of things ? The mere existence of faulty conditions is no proof of the incapacity of the government. India, for example, is admittedly a country of inexhaustible resources. It still yields an enormous revenue; its past has been one of glory and prosperity, but the present condition of the people in general may be judged from the following.

Gopal Khrishna Gokhale, a leader respected by the Indians and British alike, said in 1905 :

> Forty millions of people, according to one great Anglo-Indian authority, Sir William Hunter, pass through life with only one meal a day. According to another authority, Sir Charles Elliott, seventy millions of people in India do not know what it is to have their hunger fully satisfied, even once in the whole course of the year. The poverty of the people of India, thus considered by itself, is truly appalling. And if this is the state of things after a hundred years of your rule, you cannot claim that your principal aim in India has been the promotion of the interests of the Indian people.

Mr. Montagu, in his report on Reforms, published in 1918, says the following:

> The Indian Government compiles no statistics showing the distribution of wealth, but such incomplete figures as we have obtained show that the number of persons enjoying a substantial income is very small. In one province the total number of persons who enjoyed an income of £66 a year derived from other sources than land was 30,000; in another province 20,000. The revenue and rent returns also show how small the average agricultural holding is. According to one esti-

mate, the number of landlords whose income derived from their proprietary holdings exceeds £20 a year in the United Provinces is about 126,000, out of a population of forty-eight millions. It is evident that the curve of wealth descends very steeply, and that enormous masses of the population have little to spare for more than the necessaries of life.

Addressing an English audience, Mr. Gokhale said:

Your average annual income has been estimated at about £42 per head. Ours, according to official estimates, is about £2 per head, and according to non-official estimates, only a little more than £1 per head. Your imports per head are about £13; ours about 5s. per head. The total deposits in your Postal Savings Bank amount to 148 millions sterling, and you have in addition in the Trustees' Savings Banks about 52 millions sterling. Our Postal Savings Bank deposits, with a population seven times as large as yours, are only about 7 millions sterling, and even of this a little over one-tenth is held by Europeans. Your total paid-up capital of joint stock companies is about 1,900 millions sterling, and the greater part of this again is European. Four-fifths of our people are dependent upon agriculture, and agriculture has been for some time steadily deteriorating: Indian agriculturists are too poor, and are, moreover, too heavily indebted, to be able to apply any capital to land, and the result is that over the greater part of India agriculture is, as Sir James Caird pointed out more than twenty-five years ago, only a process of exhaustion of the soil. The yield per acre is steadily diminishing, being now about 8 to 9 bushels per acre as against about 30 bushels here in England.

In India the percentage to the whole population of children receiving education is hardly three.

Mr. Montagu, in a speech on March 7, 1919, said:

> Education is still confined to a very small minority. Industrial development is in its infancy. Does anybody in this audience realize that last year, in the great influenza epidemic, no less than six million people died in India? . . . Has not the exceptional mortality in India something to do with poverty and the consequent lack of resisting power?

When two persons are arraigned on the same charge and the evidence in each case is in effect the same, it is scarcely fair to acquit the one with honour and condemn the other with ignominy; and if explanations be forthcoming that will justify British rule in India in the face of the facts that I have just quoted, similar explanations should not be lacking in defence of Turkey. Do not let me be misunderstood. I am not seeking to condemn or disparage British rule in India. No one is more keenly alive than I to the vast and incalculable benefits that have resulted from that rule in some respects; no one can be more acutely aware, from personal knowledge and experience, of the vast and well-nigh incalculable weight of burdens of wrongs, nay, at times, even of oppression, that still remains to be lifted. Britain in all honesty and good faith has done, and is doing, her best, but the difficulties are appallingly great. India is a vast country, a continent inhabited by a variety of peoples professing different religions, speaking different languages, with manifold ideals of culture and of taste that are widely divergent. It is no easy task for a foreign government to cope with the problem of a country like this. They have done what they could.

On the other hand, a nation that has had to defend herself, to fight for her very existence on the map, for the last hundred and fifty years; that has had to face crisis after crisis under which its people have seen their unhappy country again and yet again mutilated and dismembered, could not afford to do much in the way of progress. If, as it is alleged, there has been no progress, it can be no matter for surprise, but the fault is not with that nation. She has been forced to concentrate her whole energy on strengthening her military position, and it can scarcely be denied that in that object at least she has not been unsuccessful. The Turk is admittedly a clean fighter, and a gentleman in the observance of the ethics of war. Even in the Great War this testimony has been given of him, and at the root of it all is the teaching of Islam. In the siege of Adrianople by the Bulgars in the first Balkan War, when the besieged fell short of provisions, every resident of the citadel had under the Muslim martial law to give up the extra provisions he had for the benefit of the rest; but when the Shaikh-ul-Islam heard, he at once admonished Shukri Pasha to annul the order in the case of the Zimmis, as it was contrary to the Muslim war code. The order was implicitly obeyed, and the non-Muslims retained their provisions. Whenever an expedition was sent against an enemy, the Prophet used to say: "Do not kill an old man, who is not able to fight, nor young children, nor women." Again, he admonished his general Khalid: "Do not kill any women; do not kill any labourers." It is told of Caliph Abu Bakr that he exhorted the Muslims, on their departure from Medina for the conquest of Syria, in these words: "When you meet your enemies in the fight, comport yourselves as befits good Muslims.... If God should give you the victory, do not abuse your advantage, and beware how you stain your sword in the blood of him who yields, neither touch ye the children, the women nor the infirm old men . . . cut down no palms or other fruit trees; destroy not the products of the earth, ravage not fields; burn no dwellings; from the stores of your enemies take only what you need for your wants . . . do not disturb the quiet of the monks or hermits, and destroy not their abodes."

In Jerusalem I found every place of note mentioned in the Bible preserved and protected with the same care which a Muslim holy place would demand from us. But who is responsible for the disappearance of our places of sanctity from Cordova, Toledo, Grenada, Sicily and Malta?

If the Turk has been true to his religion in such a terrible thing as war, where the shedding of human blood is commonly held of no account, could he not be true to the tenets of his religion in the government of the non-Muslims under him?

"In their anxiety for the welfare of the non-Muslim subjects, the Caliphs of Baghdad, like their rivals of Cordova, created a special department charged with the protection of the *Zimmis* and the safeguarding of their interests. The head of this department was called, in Baghdad, *Katib-ul-Jihbazeh*; in Spain, *Katib-ul-Zimam*" (*The Spirit of Islam*). Such an institution, if desirable, could well be established without any interference from outside. Even at present the non-Muslims in Turkey, if they chance to be parties in a judicial case, are given the option of being tried under their personal law. "In the year 1900, or 1901, a sub-prior of the Holy Sepulchre stole some forty thousand pounds' worth of the treasure belonging to the Armenian cathedral at Jerusalem, and tried to escape to Europe with it. He was caught at Jaffa by the Turkish customs men, taken back to Jerusalem, and, by the Governor's order, handed over to his fellow-monks for punishment, although he begged to be dealt with by the Turkish law. The Muslim government, by the constitution of the realm, he was informed, had no jurisdiction over him."[1]

Some of the facts recorded above have purposely been taken by me from the writings of the Indian Muslims who are keenly interested and are taking a leading part in the Caliphate movement in India; and their views are for that reason entitled to very careful consideration. The last two or three years since the war have seen a reign of fire and sword in Anatolia, Smyrna and Thrace. The blame lies at the door of the Greeks, yet the consciences of those who take perennial delight in tales of Turkish tyranny over non-Muslim minorities have been in no way perturbed.

Before the era of Russian intrigue, the Armenians and the Turks lived like brothers, and what Armenians did during the war, in

[1] Marmaduke Pickthall.

the Erzeroum affair, becomes a crime ten times blacker than that committed by Casement in the matter of Ireland, for which he was rightly punished.

One of the chief complaints against the Turkish rule is that it fails to "assimilate," that is to say, to absorb into its own nationality the nations over which it bears sway. The Turks are averse to such so-called assimilation, simply because they are Muslims. If assimilation by the ruling people means taking measures to exterminate people of other religions and races from the territories under its rule, or to denationalize and thus render them extinct in the course of time, as has been done by Europeans in different parts of the world, it is a thing abhorred of Islam. Leave aside the example of Spain, and consider the cases of Thessaly and Malta by way of illustration. They were to a very great extent populated by Muslims, but to-day we find there no trace of Islam. And if a person be desirous of knowing the process of "assimilation" under which the Muslim inhabitants of Sicily and Malta were dealt with, one has but to go to Salonika and see the new melting-pot for the transfusion of Muslims into Greeks. I shrink from attempting to describe the atrocious treatment to which the Muslim inhabitants are being subjected. It will not be surprising if within the course of twenty-five years more they become " assimilated " so thoroughly and in so workmanlike a fashion that no trace of a Muslim will be found there. Smyrna was also cast into the cauldron of " assimilation," and many a town in Thrace is experiencing the identical process, perhaps as an example to a cynical world of the inner significance of latter-day Christian meekness. We are proud of the Turks because they have till now abhorred the European method of " assimilation." " When the Turk governed the Morea, he did not deport or destroy the Greek population, as their statistics and their continuous history prove. After Europe handed over the Morea to the Greeks, in less than one hundred years the Muhammadan population of the Morea, formerly some 300,000, is practically nil. The same result has followed forty-three years of Hellenic liberation in Thessaly. A Muhammadan population of about 100,000 has disappeared."[1]

Had they followed the example of their Christian neighbours there would have been no Balkan States at all, and Europe, perhaps, would have been spared its storm-centre. Is it possible to cite any other Power in Europe

[1] *Fire and Sword in Asia Minor and Thrace*, p. 5.

which has displayed such humanity in its dealings with the people of other religions as Turkey? The very fact of the existence in Turkey of a great variety of creeds and nationalities, while from Spain, France, Thessaly and Malta and other regions the Muslims have entirely disappeared, goes to prove, if anything, that Turkish rule is the only rule in Europe under which people belonging to a race or religion other than those of the ruler, can live. Certain events which have occurred quite recently may seem at first sight to put a different complexion on the matter, but such is not the case. The atrocities committed by the Greeks during the last two years, in Smyrna, Thrace and neighbouring places, must of necessity tend to create that abnormal condition of mind, even in the Turk, which will goad him, if only for the moment, into emulating the horrors of the Greek savagery.

Extermination and expulsion of Muslims has been the incurable vice of Greek possession.

Although a year has not yet passed since the occupation of Eastern Thrace, and although the poor Muslims in that district—being surrounded on all sides—are deprived of a safe place to take refuge in, the number of Muslims who have emigrated under conditions of sorrow and agony amount to more than 43,000.[1]

---

[1] *Greek Atrocities in Turkey*, I, v. vi.

Massacres, pillage, outrage, fire, and crime of a hideous nature followed Greek steps in those vilayets which should have been free from the Greek brutality under a most solemn pledge given by the Prime Minister on January 5, 1918.[1] The number of the Anatolian villages that have been reduced to ashes by the Hellenic Army is more than seventy.[2] This all occurred within the last two or three years, and no one cared to take proper notice of it, though the Muslim world cried for it everywhere. On the other hand, we hear the hue and cry raised if something of a similar nature occurs to the Greek emigrants in retaliation from the other side. We read of the massacre of 10,000 Greeks nowadays in every paper. Mr. Austen Chamberlain had to get the report confirmed from the High Commissioner at Constantinople. In the poignant details of the deportation, I read with painful heart the repetition of what occurred in the region of the Dardanelles, in the vilayets of Constantinople, in Smyrna and Thrace, at the hands of the Greeks. But the blame for this all goes to that wrong policy which has been pursued since the Treaty of Sèvres. I am

[1] Nor are we fighting . . . to deprive Turkey of its capital, *or of the rich and renowned lands of Asia Minor* and Thrace, which are predominantly Turkish in race.

[2] See Appendix II.

in possession of the details of the Greek atrocities, which cannot be read by any person without shedding tears and getting his blood boiled; but I have purposely refrained from their mention here. I have only to say one word in this connection. The statesmen here should assume a most impartial attitude when dealing with these matters. This sad event cannot be made much of to affect the future policy without bringing on record the most heinous atrocities of the Greeks. We also hear that racial prejudice is cropping up in India. It can easily be averted if the statesmen here prove themselves to be above such prejudices. Let them show that the blood of a Greek is equal in their eyes to the blood of a Turk. Such an attitude only can save the critical situation and guarantee the stability of the British rule everywhere. If the nation claims to possess a strong sense of justice, let her be equitable in Greco-Ottoman affairs.

Lord Ampthill recently, in his letter to *The Times*, proposed that a deputation should be sent from Muslim India to visit Turkey and see with their own eyes the conditions there existing, form their own conclusions, and give their own views on the question. The late Governor of Madras has struck the right note here because it is with respect for the opinions and susceptibilities of the Indian Muslims that the British Government is primarily concerned in this question of the Caliphate. The one object dear to Christian hearts in England is to ensure good and just government for the Christian minorities in Turkey. No true Muslim can take exception to the demand, but there are more ways than one of acceding to it. Would not Christian minorities enjoy an eminently satisfactory mode of government if the Turks be called upon, assuming that they have hitherto failed in that duty, simply to fulfil the demands of their own religion? If they cannot, or will not, comply, then they straightway forfeit their claim to Muslim support. Could not Muslims from India be requested to use their influence with the Turks to induce them to do what is necessary on the lines of Islam? Indian Muslims who have been long associated with posts of high responsibility in the administration of their own country could without doubt discharge such a duty to the satisfaction of all.

CHAPTER XII

CONCLUSION

I HAVE refrained as far as possible from making any suggestions, but as I have seen for myself that there are very many in this country who are willing and anxious to do justice to India, I may perhaps hazard one. The administrative body here badly needs a larger proportion of the Indian element. The development of affairs since the war has made it clear that no Imperial policy can be adopted without having due regard to British policy in India. Muslim interests, for example, are admittedly extraterritorial, and cannot be delimited by frontiers. But, on the other hand, Indian labour and Indian commerce have found a home in the four corners of the world. No Imperial policy therefore will be effective if Indian interests do not receive therein the fullest consideration. You cannot, however, satisfactorily rule a nation on your own lines if the psychology of that nation be radically different from your own. Mere inability to understand has in the past caused terrible blunders of a very grave nature in India. The tragedy of Cawnpore, in 1913, is one of these. No Englishman, I believe, would willingly sanction or cause a massacre involving hundreds of lives; but the inability of the then Cawnpore District Magistrate to appreciate the Muslim sense of respect for the Mosque was primarily responsible for it. If you have to deal with the Muslim side of the Indian question, do not base your judgment solely on the opinion and knowledge of those who have been in Muslim countries in the capacity either of a ruler or a traveller. Their angle of vision can never be free from certain prejudices and prepossessions. They cannot look at things from the point of view of the subject race, and, besides, the Englishman in India has generally kept himself aloof from Indians. They make their own colonies wherever they go, and thereby obtain the minimum of opportunity for the study of the Indian life and mind. This course was followed under the mistaken impression that their prestige would thereby be enhanced—that prestige which, unfortunately, is even now crumbling to dust. They kept the Indians at arm's length, instead of making personal friends of them, and so lost the chance of making their rule popular; believing, wrongly, that force and fear could breed respect in India. The country, after all, is not devoid of the best type of nobility and culture. The Eastern is very sociable and very faithful to friendship; but British administrative policy did not avail itself of these qualities, and thought, mistakenly, that "favouritism" would secure stability of rule. Such mercenary motives make no appeal anywhere in the East. Those, and they are very few in number, who have been popular and very successful in their rule in India, even when placed among the most turbulent people, such as the Pathans, have had to strike out a new and distinct line of their own. They mixed freely with the Indians and treated them, outside the sphere of official duties, on the terms of equality. They sympathized with them as friends in their troubles, and shared in their weal and woe. Sir George Roos Keppel may be cited as a recent example. The builders of the Indian Empire were of a similar type. Much trouble has arisen from the ignorance of the Indian Civil Servants as to the social and religious conditions prevailing in India. They are unable to appreciate susceptibilities and do many things—and without any evil motive at all—which they would not have done if they had known the people fully and well. Every Civil Servant in India, besides knowing the language of the country, should also study the religion, customs and manners of the people, and the knowledge so acquired should constitute a part of his qualification before he joins the service.

This all goes to show that the administrative body needs a larger admixture of the Indian element—and that of an independent character. Moreover, such channels of information as exist are still distressingly meagre. They must be improved—that is vital. The Government here in England does not know one hundredth part of what is actually going on in India. Its attitude towards India, I am quite sure, would be very different if it only knew. Hazy knowledge and hasty inferences based upon wrong premises will not help anyone to understand the real situation and the problem which has to be faced. I am almost inclined to suggest a Bureau—quite independent and established for that one purpose—to gather information of the progress of affairs in India. No one can question the strong English sense of justice, but the measures recently adopted in India seem to have little in common with it. The fault does not lie in the judgment, but in the information on which the judgment is based. For example, when you have to deal with the Caliphate question, would it not be well first to consult those who can rightly interpret the Indian mind, and are in a position to gauge the advisability or otherwise of any measures that may be proposed? Your interest in the matter arises from the duty you owe to the Muslims in India. Why not, then, find out exactly what it is they want, and why they want it? If India is the most precious jewel in the British Crown, your interest in India should outweigh your other Imperial interests. All that has been done with regard to Turkey has simply had the effect of creating circumstances prejudicial to the British Raj and its prestige in India. The anxiety of the Viceroy, and the full conference of other provincial governors, that his dispatch to the Home Government, on the question of the Caliphate, should be published before he took the step of arresting Mahatma Gandhi is an apposite comment on what I am saying here. It does not, as certain newspapers have insinuated, show timidity on the part of the Indian Government, but is, on the contrary, a piece of true statesmanship from some points of view. On the other hand, in what way the weakening of Turkish rule can be expected to contribute to the solidarity of the British Empire is a mystery, even to many here in England. To pursue the "bag and baggage" policy of Gladstone, the narrow-mindedness of whose Christianity is by now sufficiently obvious, would simply substantiate the opinion, already current, that you cherish hostility against Islam, but that it has by a mere chance become focussed against Turkey. If the recent atrocities of the Greeks can so easily be condoned, the Premier cannot, in decency, say anything against Turkey. Neither should it be forgotten that anything done to strengthen Turkey cannot fail to strengthen British rule in the long run. It will earn the good will of the Muslim world—and that means a very great thing. Russia was once a menace to British rule in India, and if you could rely, as you did in those days, on Muslim support (and the support came spontaneously whenever it was needed), it was simply on account of the Muslim attachment to Turkey. Muslims believed you a friend to Turkey, and hated Russia because of her enmity to Turkey. Your siding with Turkey in the Crimean War, though it was of material gain to you in other ways, nevertheless endeared you to Muslim hearts. If your interests in India are in peril, what you will gain by winning the friendship of Greece at the cost of the good will of Indian Muslims is a matter still to be explained. You cannot rule India quietly without making friends with the Turk, as has very rightly been remarked by one of your best soldiers,

Sir Henry Wilson. A word from *Khalifa-tul-Muslamin*—the Turkish Sultan—to his Indian coreligionists would produce a wonderful result. As a first step in this, the right, direction, therefore, all efforts and propaganda whatsoever designed, or likely, to lower the prestige of Turkey should cease forthwith.

A side development of the Genoa Conference has left you alone to win Muslim friendship or to lose it. Sometime in 1919, before the arrival in this country of the Caliphate delegation, those working for the Caliphate movement received information from this country, through private cablegrams, that neither France nor Italy was adverse to the Muslim demands concerning Turkey, but that the whole of the opposition came from the very quarter to which Muslims had been, and not without reason, looking for support, when the question should be raised before the Allies—that is to say, from the British Government. The message, therefore, was taken by the majority of the Muslims in India to be a hasty conclusion based on erroneous information. Then came the Caliphate delegation. After about a year spent in England, France and other places, the suspicion became strengthened, and the local newspapers in India began to write on the subject with feelings not far removed from consternation at the discovery that those whom they regarded as the very protectors of their rights had become the assailants. With the return of the delegation, affairs in India assumed a grave aspect. The separate peace procured by France and Italy with Turkey has made the situation more serious. You cannot now justify any conduct adverse to Muslim interest by the plea which you advanced when Smyrna was handed over to the coming ruthless atrocities of the Greeks, namely, that you were the minority, and could not go against the decisions of the other Allies. The position is quite changed now, and understandable by the man in the street. America dissociated herself from the Allies long ago. France and Italy are not hostile to the Turks. M. Poincaré, when commenting on the Paris offer, hints at its inadequacy. The Italian Foreign Minister, Signor Schanzer, in his Genoa speech, declares that Italy is not at war with Turkey. Who, then, is at war with Turkey? And who is it that is constantly and consistently opposing the Muslim demands? The conclusion is obvious.

The only plea with any semblance of plausibility is the plea of the interests of Christian minorities. But in the first place the war was not waged with that object in view, nor, in the second, should the results of the war affect belligerents in matters religious when adherents of many religions, and especially Muslims, brought it to victory. Are not Italy and France Christian nations? What, then, makes England the chief custodian of the Christian conscience, and that, too, I fear, as a rule, only when there is nothing more serious to think about? This, for many, is a problem. I do honestly wish that people here were really sufficiently and genuinely alive in their interest in Christianity to justify Mr. Lloyd George in the policy he has selected. Again and again we hear of those empty pews which the clergy are called upon to address Sunday after Sunday. We find public houses more crowded than churches on the day of the Lord.

In such circumstances, any step now taken in pursuance of that misguided policy, in the name of Christianity, must needs be disastrous to British interests in India. Perhaps it would be asking too much for me to expect the Government to take my word for this; so I adduce the following by way of evidence:

PARIS, *Monday, May* 1.

"Unless Britain revises her Muhammadan policy the great revolution in India is inevitable."

This grave declaration was made to me yesterday by the Aga Khan, who is perhaps the greatest power of the

Muslim world. He returned this week-end from India, where he has been since November.

"What is your British policy in India?" continued his highness. "The policy should be like this race"—our conversation was taking place at Longchamps Racecourse—"at every furlong post some horse will be in front, but the object is to be in front at the last post. Is that your object in India?

"The fact that Britain, a little island in the North Sea, with a population of 33,000,000, has ruled for so long the great Empire of India, with its population of 320,000,000, 7,000 miles away, proves that you must have friends in the very soil of India.

"Your principal friends were the Muhammadans, of whom there are sixty millions. True, they are in a minority, but they were one of the roots of British rule in India, and now—now they have turned away on account of the British policy.

"You can only remain in India so long as India wills it, but you cannot govern India by giving the Garter to one man and putting another in prison.

"Lord Reading's terms, which were put forward by Mr. Montagu, were India's minimum terms, and they would have been accepted. The British Empire has had few such servants as Lord Reading and Mr. Montagu, and if Mr. Montagu ever goes to India he will have such a reception that it will prove how deep that country's affection for him is."

We then discussed other factors in the political situation in India. The Aga Khan said that 40 per cent. of the gross revenue of India was devoted to the upkeep of the Army. Taxes were too high, and people felt they were paying for the army, whose only objective is to hold India for Britain.

"In England," he said, "if you don't like a Government you can turn it out. In India, the only manner of disposing of an unpopular Government is by revolution.

"India may be quiet for two weeks, three months

or a year, but there will be more troubles unless British policy is revised."

The Aga Khan believes that the Turco-Greek situation can only be settled by giving Adrianople to the Turks. He characterized giving it to the Greeks as a "crime."

In reply to a question concerning the reported offer of the Sultan of Turkey to make reasonable terms, he said that the Sultan was the puppet of the army of occupation in Constantinople, and that he had no control over the Muhammadans.

When I asked how peace might be restored in India, the Aga Khan replied that it could be done by unburdening India of taxation for the upkeep of the Army and adopting the Reading-Montagu proposals.[1]

If the British Government is to continue in its present position—and I see no reason why it should not, as long as it rules the communities of various persuasions and beliefs under it with perfect impartiality—British statesmen should always keep in view the fact that the Muslims are in a majority under them, and are more sensitive in religious matters than any other people in the world. Steps should be taken forthwith to allay differences and disputes between Christians and Muslims in everyday civil life, at least. Islam, as I have shown, gives the most favourable conditions of government for non-Muslims, and if there are Muslim rulers who do not adhere to the law of Islam in practice, it would surely be better to compel them under the commands

[1] *Daily Express.*

of their religion to improve their ways, than to devise plans of the kind suggested by the Paris Conference, which can only serve as a perennial apple of discord, keeping the Muslim and the Christian communities at daggers drawn for all time. The developments of modern religious thought have already gone far towards bridging the great gulf hitherto fixed between Christianity and Islam. We Muslims pay the same respect to Jesus as to Muhammad : "Make no difference between prophet and prophet," is the injunction of the Qur-án. Muslims are allowed to partake of Christian food ; and we, moreover, find this in the Qur-án, the passage which brings the Christians nearer to us than the Jews : "And you will certainly find the nearest in friendship to the believers those who say, We are Christian."

The only difference between Islam and the religion of the Church is the Christian belief in the divinity of Jesus, and even here advanced thought is showing a tendency, ever stronger, towards a more and more liberal interpretation of that divinity, so much so that in the not far future it may well be that the dividing line between Islam and Christianity will become academic rather than actual. As it is, I fail to detect any essential difference on this head between the view of Islam and that put forward by the more advanced thinkers of the Church of England at last summer's Cambridge Conference. Already, indeed, such progress has been made towards a mutual understanding as would have been deemed hardly possible a century ago, and it is surely not unreasonable to hope that, if men will but keep their religion pure from the taint of politics, the day is at hand when Christian and Muslim will dwell together as brothers, each gladly recognizing in the Faith of the other a veritable branch of that Tree of Life that was in the midst of the Garden.

APPENDIX I

THE PENALTY OF APOSTASY IN ISLAM

Surely (as for) those who believe then disbelieve, again believe and again disbelieve, then increase in disbelief, Allah will not forgive them nor guide them in the (right) path. — QUR-ÁN, iv. 137.

IF there existed any doubt as to the penalty of apostasy in Islam and the fate of the apostate, the above quoted verse dispels it at once. It is clear and definite, leaving no room for discussion, requiring no comment. It speaks of one who embraces Islam and then forsakes it; who becomes a Muslim yet again, and yet again recants and becomes rooted in apostasy, while the latter part of the verse states the punishment which will be meted out to the apostate, which is that Allah will not forgive him, neither will Allah guide him any more in the path of righteousness. The offence of apostasy, like deadly sin, is to be judged by God alone, and not by human agency. Unfortunately, the rôle played by the missionary propagandist in Europe in the last century has been largely delegated to the politician, and the orgy of political blunders already perpetrated, with the effect of alienating the Muslim world from British rule is, by now, an open secret. Everyone knows that it is phil-Hellenism rather than any "dictates of humanity" which threatens the integrity of the Turkish dominion. Now that the question of the reconstruction of the Turkish Empire is under consideration by the "Near East" Conference in Paris, the "protection of minorities under the Turk" shibboleth may lead to many issues, of which one may very possibly turn on the penalty erroneously supposed to attach to apostasy in Islam; and a word or two on this subject would seem to be therefore not only advisable, but most necessary.

Muslims take their religion from the Qur-án and from the actions of the Prophet Muhammad, and these latter are only followed by way of practical explanation of the former. "My words cannot abrogate the words of God; but the words of God can abrogate mine." So says the Noble Prophet.

The sole test of authenticity to be applied to his own words is the Qur-án; and it is to the Qur-án therefore that we must look to discover the penalty for apostasy. The verse I have quoted makes no mention of any actual punishment in a material sense. A return to unbelief after belief is mentioned more than once, and neither death nor any other human punishment is so much as hinted at. In two other passages the Qur-án treats of apostasy, and in these the very word *Irtitad* has been used, which bears the technical significance of apostasy. One of them is the 54th verse of the fifth chapter, which I quote from Muhammad Ali's translation:

> O you who believe! *whoever from among you turns back from his religion, then Allah will bring a people,* He shall love them and they shall love Him; lowly before the believers, mighty against the unbelievers, they shall strive hard in Allah's way and shall not fear the censure of any censurer; this is Allah's grace, He gives it to whom He pleases, and Allah is Ample-giving, Knowing.

The verse speaks of no penalty for the renegades from Islam, but tells by way of prophecy that apostasy will be followed by the coming of a better people into the fold of Islam. In Chapter II, the concluding portion of verse 217 speaks thus of apostasy:

And whoever of you turns back from his religion, *then he dies while an unbeliever*—these it is whose works shall go for nothing in this world, and the hereafter, and they are the inmates of the fire; therein they shall abide.

I append Sale's translation of the same verse:

Whoever among you shall turn back from his religion, and die an infidel, their works shall be vain in this world, and the next; they shall be the companions of hell-fire, they shall remain therein for ever.

And Rodwell's version is in nearly the same words. The penalty to the apostate is not death but, in the translation of Rodwell, "their works shall be fruitless in this world and in the next," and in the rendering of Sale, "their works shall be vain in this world and the next." Then comes the punishment in the life after death, "They shall be the companions of hell-fire." I do not find any other mention of apostasy in the Qur-án, and certainly nothing to justify the suggestion that death is, or ever was, the penalty of apostasy in Islam. The miseonstruction or misinterpretation of Islam seems, unfortunately, to have fallen to the lot of certain Christian writers, and in this verse the word *Fayamut* has given them their opportunity. Muhammad Ali translates it, "then he dies while an unbeliever"; Sale, "and die an infidel"; and Rodwell, "and die an infidel." But the Christian propagandist has translated it "he shall be put to death." This is not only a gross misinterpretation on his part, but evinees, if intended sincerely, his utter ignoranee of the Arabic language. Sale, whose maligning-Islam tendeneies are well known, could hardly have failed to make mueh of it if the verse had allowed him the least latitude.

In the days of the Prophet all the reliable reeords of his life are silent on the subjeet. There were many apostasies doubtless, but no one was punished, for it is, and has ever been, the watehword of Islam that there shall be "no compulsion in religion" (ii. 256). We, however, read of the putting to death of the party of 'Ukl in our traditions, who, after professing Islam, feigned that the climate of Medina was insalubrious, and being told to go to the place where the herds of camels belonging to the State were grazed, murdered the keepers and drove the herds along with them. They were charged under the crime of murder and dacoity, for which the punishment of death has been provided in ch. v. 33. This episode has generally been cited by the Qur-ánic commentators under the verse which ordains the death penalty for murder and dacoity; and there is no other case which can even be twisted to show that the punishment of death was ever inflicted on apostasy from Islam.

Reference may be made to wrong actions on the part of subsequent followers of Islam who assumed the garb of religion merely to further their political aims; but this is not peculiar to Muslims. Has not the modern politician most infelicitously compared the recent fighting in the neighbourhood of Jerusalem with the Crusades, and gone so far as to hail Salonika as the gate of Christianity? If Christianity is not responsible for the horrors of the Inquisition, before which the horrors of hell fade into insignificance, wrongs done by some few Muslim zealots, if done against the clear teachings of the Qur-án, cannot be put to the account of Islam. The deliberators of the Paris Conference should bear in mind that if this supposed death penalty for apostasy in Islam is to be used as a pretext for tampering with the authority of the Sultan, it will amount to nothing more nor less than an uncalled-for attack on our religion. We take it as an insult and a slur on our religion, and the phil-Hellenists should think twice before they allow the question of apostasy to influence their decision. Let us have no more blunders. We Muslims do believe in freedom of conscience, and we do denounce the action of a Muslim government even under which capital punishment is meted against apostasy. The Book which says, " All Muslims, Jews, Christians and Sabians who believe in God and the last day, and do good works, shall have their reward with their Lord " (Qur-án ii. 59) —such cannot allow its followers to look with hatred towards Christians and Jews, no matter if they be so by birth or are renegades from Islam. Islam is the proverbial enemy of idolatry, the sworn foe of polytheism in every form. Yet millions of temples, pagodas and shrines, consecrated to numberless gods, goddesses and demi-gods, teeming with valuable golden and marble images and idols, have survived the most triumphant rule of Islam in India. They still possess the artistic beauty and sublimity of the ancient workmanship, and excite the wonder of the modern craftsman. Does not this fact speak highly of that largeness of soul which the holy texts have infused into the notorious breakers of idols ? But where are the remains of our art and culture in places which were taken from us by the Christians of Spain ?

APPENDIX II

THE ANATOLIAN VILLAGES BURNT BY THE HELLENIC ARMY

THE following are the names of seventy villages that the Greeks have reduced to ashes:

Ghidil, Démirdji, Oglakdji, Khortou, Kodjash, Kadindjik, Holanti, Bourma, Aïvali, Merdjan, Yari-Yayla, Gheruler-Yaylassi, Tahtali-Tatar-Keuy, Karié-Oghlou, Saray-Keuy, Ghunduzler, Kizildja-Euren, Osmanié, Agha-Pinar, Aghir-Euren, Utch-Bashli, Eumer-Keuy, Sazak, Yarikdji, Belen, Daghdji, Messoudié, Kara-Viran, Has-Keuy, Mihalidjik-Kassabassi, Fozatch, Tchankdji, Kara-Hamza, Yildiz, Baghtché-djik, Zindjirli-Kouyou, Merdjan, Halil-Oghlan, Sherefli, Yeni-Mehmed, Tchélikli, Soghoudjali, Kaltakli, Kour-sakli, Sébil-Sufla, Sari-Keuy, Ortaklar, Koushdjaghiz, Iydedjik, Bol, Yaka-Kaya, Kaymaz-Kizi, Oula-Néfili, Ghuzéldjé-Kala, Katrandji, Loutfié, Halil-Oghlan, Gheuk-Keuy, Koyou-Yalassi, Gheukdje-Ayva, Kizli-Yurekli, Iydé-Aghatch, Bilédjik-Kassabassi, Alpo, Mamouré, Yéshil-Don, Otouz-Hamam, Eski-Tchalish, Sépédji.

According to the report of the delegate of the Red Crescent who accompanied the international inquiry mission into the regions of Samanli-Dagh and of Yalova, the following villages have been entirely burnt by the Greeks:

Ghadjik, Déré-Keuy, Sultanié, Kara-Kilissa, Yortan, Kirazli, Safoudjouk, Pasha-Keuy, Koirt-Keuy, Gheudjé-Déré, Eudez-Pinar, Orta-Bouroun, Kélék, Tchalidja, Réshadié, the farm of Sukri-Effendi (near Yalova).

APPENDIX III

THE MINORITIES

THE populations of districts referred to are appended :—

	Total Population.	Muslims.	Per cent.
ASIA MINOR			
"Cilicia" (Adana and part of Aleppo)	920,583	755,541	82
"Armenia" (Trebizonde, Erzeroum, Van and Bitlis)	2,522,027	1,812,790	71
"Smyrna" Province	1,397,477	1,093,334	78
Rest of Asia Minor	7,414,776	6,200,618	83
TURKEY IN EUROPE			
E. and W. Thrace and Constantinople	2,343,214	1,502,862	64

APPENDIX IV

WRITTEN STATEMENT OF MAHATMA GANDHI [1]

I OWE it perhaps to the Indian public and to the public in England, to placate which this prosecution is mainly taken up, that I should explain why from a staunch loyalist and co-operator I have become an uncompromising disaffectionist and non-co-operator. To the court too I should say why I plead guilty to the charge of promoting disaffection towards the government established by law in India.

My public life began in 1893 in South Africa in troubled weather. My first contact with British authority in that country was not of a happy character. I discovered that as a man and an Indian I had no rights. On the contrary, I discovered that I had no rights as a man because I was an Indian.

But I was not baffled. I thought that this treatment of Indians was an excrescence upon a system that was intrinsically and mainly good. I gave the government my voluntary and hearty co-operation, criticizing it fully where I felt it was faulty, but never wishing its destruction.

Consequently, when the existence of the Empire was threatened in 1899 by the Boer challenge, I offered my services to it, raised a volunteer ambulance corps

---

[1] Read by him on March 18, 1922, in the Court of Mr. Broomfield, District and Sessions Judge of Ahmedabad. (Taken from *The Great Trial of Mahatma Gandhi and Mr. Banker*. Published by Ganesh & Co., Publishers, Madras.)

and served at several actions that took place for the relief of Ladysmith. Similarly in 1906, at the time of the Zulu revolt, I raised a stretcher-bearer party and served till the end of the "rebellion." On both these occasions I received medals and was even mentioned in dispatches. For my work in South Africa I was given by Lord Hardinge a Kaiser-i-Hind Gold Medal. When the war broke out in 1914 between England and Germany, I raised a volunteer ambulance corps in London, consisting of the then resident Indians in London, chiefly students. Its work was acknowledged by the authorities to be valuable. Lastly, in India, when a special appeal was made at the War Conference in Delhi in 1917 by Lord Chelmsford for recruits, I struggled at the cost of my health to raise a corps in Kheda, and the response was being made when the hostilities ceased and orders were received that no more recruits were wanted. In all these efforts at service I was actuated by the belief that it was possible by such services to gain a status of full equality in the Empire for my countrymen.

The first shock came in the shape of the Rowlatt Act, a law designed to rob the people of all real freedom. I felt called upon to lead an intensive agitation against it. Then followed the Punjab horrors, beginning with the massacre at Jallianwala Bagh and culminating in crawling orders, public floggings and other indescribable humiliations. I discovered, too, that the plighted word of the Prime Minister to the Mussulmans of India, regarding the integrity of Turkey and the Holy Places of Islam, was not likely to be fulfilled. But in spite of the foreboding and the grave warnings of friends, at the Amritsar Congress in 1919 I fought for co-operation and working the Montagu-Chelmsford reforms, hoping that the Prime Minister would redeem his promise to the Indian Mussulmans, that the Punjab wound would be healed and that the reforms, inadequate and unsatisfactory though they were, marked a new era of hope in the life of India.

But all that hope was shattered. The Caliphate promise was not to be redeemed. The Punjab crime was whitewashed, and most culprits went not only unpunished but remained in service, and some continued to draw pensions from the Indian revenue, and in some cases were even rewarded. I saw, too, that not only did the reforms not mark a change of heart, but they were only a method of further draining India of her wealth and of prolonging her servitude.

I came reluctantly to the conclusion that the British connection had made India more helpless than she ever was before, politically and economically. A disarmed India has no power of resistance against any aggressor if she wanted to engage in an armed conflict with him. So much is this the case that some of our best men consider that India must take generations before she can achieve the Dominion status. She has become so poor that she has little power of resisting famines. Before the British advent India spun and wove in her millions of cottages just the supplement she needed for adding to her meagre agricultural resources. The cottage industry, so vital for India's existence, has been ruined by incredibly heartless and inhuman processes, as described by English witnesses. Little do town-dwellers know how the semi-starved masses of Indians are slowly sinking to lifelessness. Little do they know that their miserable comfort represents the brokerage they get for the work they do for the foreign exploiter, that the profits and the brokerage are sucked from the masses. Little do they realize that the government established by law in British India is carried on for this exploitation of the masses. No sophistry, no jugglery in figures can explain away the evidence the skeletons in many villages present to the naked eye. I have no doubt whatsoever that both England and the town-dwellers of India will have to answer, if there is a God above, for this crime against humanity, which is perhaps unequalled in history. The law itself in this country has been used to serve the foreign exploiter.

My unbiased examination of the Punjab Martial Law cases has led me to believe that at least 95 per cent. of convictions were wholly bad. My experience of political cases in India leads me to the conclusion that in nine out of every ten the condemned men were totally innocent. Their crime consisted in love of their country. In ninety-nine cases out of a hundred justice has been denied to Indians as against Europeans in the Court of India. This is not an exaggerated picture. It is the experience of almost every Indian who has had anything to do with such cases. In my opinion, the administration of the law is thus prostituted consciously or unconsciously for the benefit of the exploiter.

The greatest misfortune is that Englishmen and their Indian associates in the administration of the country do not know that they are engaged in the crime I have attempted to describe. I am satisfied that many English and Indian officials honestly believe that they are administering one of the best systems devised in the world and that India is making steady though slow progress. They do not know that a subtle but effective system of terrorism and an organized display of force on the one hand, and the deprivation of all powers of retaliation or self-defence on the other, have emasculated the people and induced in them the habit of simulation. This awful habit has added to the ignorance and the self-deception of the administrators. Section 124 A, under which I am happily charged, is perhaps the prince among the political sections of the Indian Penal Code, designed to suppress the liberty of the citizen. Affection cannot be manufactured or regulated by law. If one has no affection for a person or thing, one should be free to give the fullest expression to his disaffection so long as he does not contemplate, promote or incite to violence. But the section under which Mr. Banker and I are charged is one under which mere promotion of disaffection is a crime. I have studied some of the cases tried under it, and I know that some of the most loved of India's patriots have been convicted under it. I consider it a privilege, therefore, to be charged under it. I have endeavoured to give in their briefest outline the reasons for my disaffection. I have no personal ill-will against any single administrator, much less can I have any disaffection towards the King's person. But I hold it to be a virtue to be disaffected towards a government which in its totality has done more harm to India than any previous system. India is less manly under the British rule than she ever was before. Holding such a belief, I consider it to be a sin to have affection for the system. And it has been a precious privilege for me to be able to write what I have in the various articles tendered in evidence against me.

In fact, I believe that I have rendered a service to India and England by showing in non-co-operation the way out of the unnatural state in which both are living. In my humble opinion, non-co-operation with evil is as much a duty as is co-operation with good. But in the past, non-co-operation has been deliberately expressed in violence to the evildoer. I am endeavouring to show to my countrymen that violent non-co-operation only multiplies evil, and that as evil can only be sustained by violence, withdrawal of support of evil requires complete abstention from violence. Non-violence implies voluntary submission to the penalty for non-co-operation with evil. I am here, therefore, to invite and submit cheerfully to the highest penalty that can be inflicted upon me for what in law is a deliberate crime and what appears to me to be the highest duty of a citizen. The only course open to you, the Judge and the Assessors, is either to resign your posts and thus dissociate yourselves from evil, if you feel that the law you are called upon to administer is an evil and that in reality I am innocent, or to inflict on me the severest penalty if you believe that the system and the law you are assisting to administer are good for the people of this country and that my activity is therefore injurious to the public weal.

APPENDIX V

CHRISTIAN OFFICIALS IN THE TURKISH ADMINISTRATION

The following few names have been taken from the Ottoman Civil List, and do not include different officers belonging to various Christian nationalities who served as Judges, Administrators, Governors, Sub-Governors, Chiefs of Sections in various State Departments, Secretaries, Senior Officers in the Army, etc.

Musurus Pasha (Greek), Vézir, Ambassador in London. Alexandre Carathéodory Pasha (Greek), Vézir, Minister of Foreign Affairs. Agop Pasha (Armenian), Vézir, Minister of Finances. Franco Pasha (Catholic), Vézir, Governor. Aleco Pasha (Bulgarian), Vézir, Ambassador and Governor-General. Gavril Pasha (Bulgarian), Vézir, Governor-General. Photiades Pasha (Greek), Vézir, Ambassador. Rustem Pasha (Catholic), Vézir, Ambassador. Savas Pasha (Greek), Vézir, Minister of Foreign Affairs. Ohannès Pasha Sakiz (Armenian), Vézir, Minister of the Civil List of His Imperial Majesty the Sultan. Artin Pasha Dadian (Armenian), Vézir, Under-Secretary of State for Foreign Affairs. Naoum Pasha (Catholic), Vézir, Governor-General and Ambassador. Mouzaffer Pasha (Catholic), Vézir, Governor-General. Portocal Michael Pasha (Armenian), Vézir, Minister of the Civil List of His Imperial Majesty the Sultan. Youssouf Pasha Franco (Catholic), Vézir, Minister of Foreign Affairs. Vassa Pasha (Catholic), Vézir, Governor-General. Costaki Anthopoulos Pasha (Greek), Vézir, Ambassador. Musurus Pasha (son of Musurus Pasha at the head of this list), (Greek), Vézir, Ambassador in London. Mavroyéni Pasha (Greek), Vézir, High Official of His Imperial Majesty's Palace. Couyoumdjian Ohannès Pasha (Armenian), Vézir, Governor-General. Couyoumdjian Bedros Effendi (Armenian), Minister of Mines and Forests. Mavroyéni Bey (Greek), Senator and Ambassador. Aristidi Pasha (Greek), Vézir, Minister of Commerce and Agriculture. Gabriel Effendi Noradounghian (Armenian), Minister of Foreign Affairs, at present Leader of the Armenian Committee. Tchamidj Ohannes Effendi (Armenian), President at the Ministry of Finances. Abro Effendi (Armenian), Councillor of State. Constantin Caratheodory Effendi (Greek), Councillor of State. Aram Effendi (Armenian), Senator. Azarian Effendi (Armenian), Minister Plenipotentiary, Under-Secretary of State for Foreign Affairs, Senator. Herand Bey Abro (Armenian), Legal Adviser of the Sublime Porte. Ohan Effendi (Armenian), Under-Secretary of State for the Ministry of Justice. Fethi Bey Franco (Catholic), Under-Secretary of State for Foreign Affairs.

Printed in Great Britain by

UNWIN BROTHERS, LIMITED, THE GRESHAM PRESS, LONDON AND WOKING